What is Teaching
in the Lifelong Learning Sector?

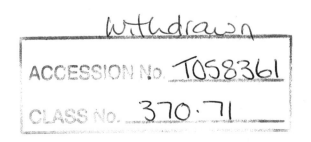

What is Teaching
in the Lifelong Learning Sector?

Ann Gravells

Los Angeles | London | New Delhi
Singapore | Washington DC

Published by Learning Matters
An imprint of SAGE Publications Ltd
1 Oliver's Yard
55 City Road
London EC1Y 1SP

SAGE Publications Inc.
2455 Teller Road
Thousand Oaks, California 91320

SAGE Publications India Pvt Ltd
B 1/11 Mohan Cooperative Industrial Area
Mathura Road
New Delhi 110 044

SAGE Publications Asia-Pacific Pte Ltd
3 Church Street
#10-04 Samsung Hub
Singapore 049483

Editor: Amy Thornton
Development editor: Jennifer Clark
Production controller: Chris Marke
Production management: Deer Park Productions,
Tavistock, Devon
Marketing manager: Catherine Slinn
Cover design: Topics
Typeset by: PDQ Typesetting, Newcastle-under-Lyme
Printed by: TJ International, Padstow, Cornwall

Library of Congress Control Number 2012933582

British Library Cataloguing in Publication data

A catalogue record for this book is available from
the British Library

ISBN 978 0 85725 856 4
ISBN 978 0 85725 729 1 (pbk)

CONTENTS

Ann Gravells is a lecturer in teacher training at Bishop Burton College in East Yorkshire and a consultant to The University of Cambridge's Institute of Continuing Education's Assessment Network. She has been teaching since 1983.

She is an external quality consultant for the City & Guilds teacher training qualifications, a presenter of events and a consultant for various other projects.

Ann is a director of her own company *Ann Gravells Ltd*, an educational consultancy which specialises in teaching, training and quality assurance. She delivers events and courses nationwide.

Ann holds a Masters in Educational Management, a PGCE, a degree in Education, and a City & Guilds Medal of Excellence for teaching. Ann is a Fellow of the Institute for Learning and holds QTLS status.

She is often asked how her surname should be pronounced. The 'vells' part of Gravells is pronounced like 'bells'.

Ann is the author of:

- *Achieving your TAQA Assessor and Internal Quality Assurer Award*
- *Delivering Employability Skills in the Lifelong Learning Sector*
- *Passing PTLLS Assessments*
- *Preparing to Teach in the Lifelong Learning Sector*
- *Principles and Practice of Assessment in the Lifelong Learning Sector*
- *What is Teaching in the Lifelong Learning Sector?*

co-author of:

- *Equality and Diversity in the Lifelong Learning Sector*
- *Passing CTLLS Assessments*
- *Planning and Enabling Learning in the Lifelong Learning Sector*

and has edited:

- *Study Skills for PTLLS*

The author welcomes any comments from readers. Please contact her via her website:

www.anngravells.co.uk

ACKNOWLEDGEMENTS

I would like to thank the following for their support and contributions while writing this book:

Sharon Abbott, Peter Adeney, Suzanne Blake, Marie Falconer, Angela Faulkner, Susan Mullins, Cathryn O'Donovan and Mel Page.

I am particularly grateful for the guidance provided by Richard Malthouse, who kept me up to date with changes and developments in the sector.

I would also like to thank my father Bob Gravells for his excellent proofreading skills. Also, my husband Peter Frankish, who never complains about the amount of time I spend in the office writing. Also my editor Jennifer Clark, and Amy Thornton from Learning Matters, who are always at the end of the phone when I feel under pressure and need motivation and encouragement.

Ann Gravells

April 2012

www.anngravells.co.uk

Introduction

In this chapter you will learn about the:
- purpose of the book
- historical perspective
- Qualifications and Credit Framework

Purpose of the book

This book is aimed at anyone who is considering entering, or has recently entered, the Lifelong Learning Sector (LLS) as a teacher, tutor, trainer, instructor or lecturer. The LLS is also known as:

- Further Education (FE)

- Post Compulsory Education and Training (PCET)

- Adult and Continuing Education (ACE)

and traditionally involved those aged 16 and upwards. The LLS now includes individuals aged 14 and above, as younger students partake in vocational programmes which are often taught in other organisations besides schools.

There are many abbreviations and acronyms used within the sector and you will find most of these listed in Appendix 1. The first occurrence of each will always be written in full in each chapter. Appendix 2 contains some useful frequently asked questions (FAQs) from new and intending teachers to the Lifelong Learning Sector.

The content of the chapters will help you understand more about the sector and give you an insight about what it's like to teach and assess students. For the purpose of this book, the generic term *teacher* is used, even though you might be called something different, such as assessor, coach, counsellor, facilitator, instructor, lecturer, mentor, trainer or tutor. The generic term *student* is used and also refers to other terms such as apprentice, candidate, learner, participant, pupil or trainee. The term *programme* is used to denote a course which may be of any length, either leading to a qualification or for general interest.

Depending upon what you will teach and your job role, you may be required to obtain a specific award or qualification, for example, the:

- Award in Preparing to Teach in the Lifelong Learning Sector (PTLLS)
- Certificate in Teaching in the Lifelong Learning Sector (CTLLS)
- Diploma in Teaching in the Lifelong Learning Sector (DTLLS)

Higher Education Institutions still use the term *Certificate in Education (Cert Ed)* even though the content is the same as the DTLLS Diploma. There is also a *Professional Graduate Certificate in Education* and a *Postgraduate Certificate in Education (PGCE)*, which again cover the same content as DTLLS but are offered at higher levels. Further information regarding the teaching qualifications can be found in Chapter 2.

The professional body for teachers in the Lifelong Learning Sector is called The Institute for Learning (IfL) and you may like to register with them to gain all the benefits of being a member, even if you are not yet teaching. All teachers and trainers working in publicly funded further education and skills provision in England are required to register as members of IfL.

The chapters contain examples of situations that can occur in the sector, along with activities for you to carry out to help you consider what it's like to teach. The book is generic and not *subject specific*, i.e. it is not related to the subject you would like to teach. You are responsible for being knowledgeable and/or experienced in your subject, known as an *area of specialism* or *specialist subject*. You must also keep up to date with any changes and developments in your subject area; this is known as continuing professional development (CPD). You will be able to find out what the requirements are to teach your subject by contacting the relevant Sector Skills Council (SSC) or Standard Setting Body (SSB). There will be a Council or Body responsible for your particular subject and a quick search via the internet should establish yours. You can then contact them to find out what qualifications and/or experience you need to teach your subject.

Some chapters contain information from the book *Preparing to Teach in the Lifelong Learning Sector: The New Award* (2012), also by Ann Gravells.

At the end of each chapter is a theory focus containing references and further information to enable you to research relevant topics by using textbooks, publications and the internet. The index at the back of the book will quickly help you to locate relevant topics.

Historical perspective

Working within the education sector you will experience perpetual change, not only regarding your job role, but also due to local and government initiatives, including funding, legislation, skills deficits and qualification revisions. This section will give you a brief historical perspective regarding teacher training in England. There are slight differences for the other United Kingdom nations.

Historically, unlike school teachers, teachers in the Lifelong Learning Sector did not require teaching qualifications. In the 1960s the Postgraduate Certificate in Education (PGCE) became the main teacher training qualification; however, this was primarily for teachers in schools. It was often taken at a teacher training college or university after achieving a degree. It was followed in the 1970s by the Further Education Teachers' Certificate (FETC), which could be achieved through organisations offering City and Guilds qualifications. It was commonly known by the number 730 and was followed in the 1980s by a work-based National Vocational Qualification (NVQ) known by the number 7306. The 730 was then revised and became known as the 7307. Another awarding organisation at the time, The Royal Society of Arts (now known as Oxford, Cambridge and RSA Examinations), also offered their versions of the teaching certificate. Throughout all this time, the Certificate in Education was still available. Other awarding organisations also began to offer teacher training qualifications but none were government regulated and there was no requirement for teachers of adults to gain a qualification. The National Council for Vocational Qualifications (NCVQ) was established in 1986 as a result of a White Paper, *Working Together: Education and Training* (1986) to co-ordinate training, education and qualifications for all people to ensure a competent workforce in Britain for the twenty-first century.

NCVQ stated that further education teachers involved with the delivery and assessment of National Vocational Qualifications (NVQs) should be qualified. The Training and Development Lead Body (TDLB) was established in 1990 to write standards for various teaching roles. In 1992, The Further Education Unit (FEU) completed trials of the TDLB standards to explore the relevance of these to staff in further education, and recommended they should be used as a basis for teacher training. The standards were revised and incorporated into the Further Education National Training Organisation (FENTO) standards in 1999. In 2000 the Department for Education and Employment (DfEE) issued a consultation paper, *Compulsory Teaching Qualifications for Teachers in Further Education* (DfEE 2000). Although many lecturers in colleges who taught academic subjects were well qualified with a subject degree and a teaching qualification, teachers of vocational subjects often were not. However, it was not until 2001 that it became mandatory for all further education teachers in England and Wales to work towards a teaching qualification, regardless of their job role.

In November 2002, the DfES published *Success for all – reforming further education and training*. This set out targets for all full-time and part-time further education teachers to be qualified and emphasised the importance of good specialist subject knowledge.

In 2003, an Office for Standards in Education (Ofsted) survey found the current system of further education teacher training did not provide a satisfactory foundation of professional development for teachers. It questioned whether the FENTO standards were appropriate in setting the requirements for newly qualified teachers and concluded they were not. It also recommended the standards would benefit from substantial revision.

A Licence to Practise (2004) identified the components of a licence to teach for qualified teachers in the learning and skills sector. This was based upon the findings of the 2003 Ofsted survey and *The future of initial teacher education for the learning and skills sector – an agenda for reform – a consultative paper* (2003). Both reports and the subsequent consultation events triggered considerable discussion about a suitable model of teacher training to supply effective teachers in the diverse and developing Lifelong Learning Sector.

In 2004, Lifelong Learning UK (LLUK) was established and revised the FENTO standards. Development of the standards represented the first step in the construction of a new Framework of Qualifications relating to the job roles of teachers in the Lifelong Learning Sector. Further information regarding the qualifications can be found in Chapter 2.

LLUK produced a proposal for developing a *threshold* qualification for teachers to address the DfES strategy in *Equipping our Teachers for the Future* (2004). LLUK had a remit to develop a *Preparing to Teach in the Lifelong Learning Sector (PTLLS) Award* by May 2006, ready for piloting in September 2006. Teachers would then progress to the *Certificate in Teaching in the Lifelong Learning Sector* (CTLLS) or the *Diploma in Teaching in the Lifelong Learning Sector* (DTLLS) depending upon their job role. These qualifications are still current, having been revised in 2011/12 and are made up of units, some mandatory and others optional. Standards Verification UK (SVUK), a subsidiary of LLUK, was given the remit of endorsing all Initial Teacher Training (ITT) qualifications to ensure they met the requirements in the Framework. Achievement of the relevant qualification, along with actual teaching, should ensure the required teaching standards are met.

In 2007, the Further Education Teaching Regulations (England) came into force. It became mandatory for all new teachers who teach in further education (and on programmes receiving government funding) to become qualified within five years of commencing their post. Existing teachers who were already suitably qualified prior to this date and who fulfilled the FENTO requirements did not need to take the new qualifications. There were also compulsory requirements for teachers to demonstrate continuing professional development (CPD) annually and to register with the Institute for Learning (IfL). Currently there is a cost to be a member of the IfL.

The Learning and Skills Improvement Service (LSIS) is now responsible for the teacher training standards, having taken over from LLUK and SVUK in 2011. However, there may be changes in the future due to further government department restructures.

This book was published prior to the Lord Lingfield Report *Professionalism in Further Education* and there may have been some changes to the requirements for teachers in the Lifelong Learning sector as a result.

Qualifications and Credit Framework

The Qualifications and Credit Framework (QCF) and Scottish Credit and Qualifications Framework (SCQF) are systems for recognising skills and qualifications. The QCF was piloted in 2006 and became fully operational in 2011. The QCF simplifies the way units and qualifications are recognised by giving them a title of Award, Certificate or Diploma. This should make recognising qualifications a lot easier, for example, by employers when recruiting new staff. There have been many different titles in the past, such as National Vocational Qualifications (NVQ), Higher National Certificates (HNC) and Vocational Qualifications (VQ) etc. It will take a few more years for the titles of Award, Certificate and Diploma to be fully understood and recognised; however, it will make it easier to see what someone has achieved. The flexibility of the system allows students to gain qualifications at their own pace along routes that suit them best. The QCF uses the term *learner* rather than *student*.

Levels

The QCF has 9 levels; entry level plus 1 to 8 (there are 12 levels on the Scottish Framework). The level refers to the difficulty of the skills, knowledge and understanding required to achieve the qualification.

A rough comparison of the levels to existing qualifications is:

1 – GCSEs (grades D–G)
2 – GCSEs (grade A*–C)
3 – A levels
4 – Vocational Qualification (VQ) level 4, Higher National Certificate (HNC)
5 – NVQ level 5, Degree, Higher National Diploma (HND)
6 – Honours degree
7 – Masters degree
8 – Doctor of Philosophy (PhD)

It is anticipated that all qualifications will be amended to fit into the framework and it is hoped there will be a European framework and eventually a worldwide framework. This will make the recognition of qualifications much easier for people applying for jobs internationally.

Units

Qualifications on the Framework are broken down into units (small steps of learning) and each unit has a credit value. This credit value specifies the number of hours it would take an average person to complete the qualification, with one credit equalling ten hours. For example, the Award in Preparing to Teach in the Lifelong Learning Sector (PTLLS) is 12 credits, which equates to 120 hours of learning. The hours include *contact time* with a teacher and assessor, and *non-contact time* for individual study, assignment work and the production of a portfolio of evidence.

All qualifications on the QCF use the terms *learning outcomes* and *assessment criteria*. The learning outcomes state what the learner *will do*, and the assessment criteria what the learner *can do*.

The content of the learning outcomes is the same if a unit is offered at different levels; the difference is expressed in the skills and knowledge required for achievement. For example, if you are taking a level 3 you will *explain* how or why you do something, at level 4 you will *analyse* how or why you do it. If you are working towards a level 4 unit you will need to carry out relevant research and correctly reference your work to theorists and texts.

For example, the first PTLLS unit, called *Roles, Responsibilities and Relationships in Lifelong Learning*, contains three learning outcomes which are offered at both level 3 and level 4. The first learning outcome and associated assessment criteria are shown in Table 1.1. You can see how some of the assessment criteria are different at level 4, to reflect the fact that more work will be required to achieve the learning outcome.

If you are going to teach towards a qualification, it is highly likely it will be displayed in the format of *learning outcomes* and *assessment criteria*. You would use these as the starting point for devising what will be taught and how it will be assessed.

Size

There are three sizes of qualifications with titles and associated credit values:

Award (1 to 12 credits)
Certificate (13 to 36 credits)
Diploma (37 credits or more)

Table 1.1 – PTLLS unit: *Roles, Responsibilities and Relationships in Lifelong Learning*

Learning Outcome *The learner will:*	Assessment Criteria Level 3 *The learner can:*		Assessment Criteria Level 4 *The learner can:*	
1. Understand own role and responsibilities in lifelong learning	1.1	Summarise key aspects of legislation, regulatory requirements and codes of practice relating to own role and responsibilities	1.1	Summarise key aspects of legislation, regulatory requirements and codes of practice relating to own role and responsibilities
	1.2	Explain own responsibilities for equality and valuing diversity	1.2	Analyse own responsibilities for promoting equality and valuing diversity
	1.3	Explain own role and responsibilities in lifelong learning	1.3	Evaluate own role and responsibilities in lifelong learning
	1.4	Explain own role and responsibilities in identifying and meeting the needs of learners	1.4	Review own role and responsibilities in identifying and meeting the needs of learners

The terms Award, Certificate and Diploma do not relate to progression, i.e. you don't start with an Award, progress to the Certificate and then to the Diploma. The terms relate to how big the qualification is (i.e. its size), which is based on the total number of credits (i.e. number of hours it takes to complete). The level will define how difficult it is, for example level 4 will be more difficult to achieve than level 3 and so on.

Purpose

All qualifications on the QCF have a *purpose*, i.e. the reason it can be offered. The purpose of the teaching qualifications is *Confirm occupational competence and/or licence to practise*. If you are teaching a qualification which is on the QCF, it will have a purpose of which there are five:

A Recognise personal growth and engagement in learning
B Prepare for further learning or training and/or develop knowledge and/or skills in a subject area
C Prepare for employment
D Confirm occupational competence and/or licence to practise
E Updating and continuing professional development (CPD).

The responsibility for the regulation of the QCF lies with Ofqual, together with its partner regulators in Wales (DCELLS) and Northern Ireland (CCEA). There is a separate framework for Scotland. The frameworks will eventually contain all available qualifications and include school qualifications such as the current General Certificate of Secondary Education (GCSE) and Advanced Level certificates (A levels).

Unique Learner Numbers

When a student commences their first qualification on the QCF they will be given a *unique learner number* (ULN) or *Scottish candidate number* (SCN) in Scotland, which they will keep for life. This number will be used to track all achievements and can be used by the student to view their record online. More information regarding the QCF website can be found at the shortcut http://tinyurl.com/447bgy2

Summary

In this chapter you have learnt about:

● the purpose of the book

● the historical perspective

● the Qualifications and Credit Framework

Theory focus

References and further information

Clarke, C (2002) *Success For All – Reforming Further Education and Training – Our Vision for the Future.* London: DFES.

DfES (1986) White Paper, *Working Together: Education and Training.* London: HMSO.

DfES (2003) *The future of initial teacher education for the learning and skills sector – an agenda for reform – a consultative paper.* London: DfES.

DfES (2004) *Equipping our teachers for the future: Reforming initial teacher training for the learning and skills sector.* London: DfES Standards Unit.

DfES (2005) FE White Paper, *Raising Skills, Improving Life Chances.* London: DfES.

FENTO (1999) *Standards for teaching and supporting learning in further education in England and Wales.* London: FENTO.

Gravells, A (2012) *Preparing to Teach in the Lifelong Learning Sector: The New Award* (5th edition). Exeter: Learning Matters.

LLUK (2006) *New overarching professional standards for teachers, tutors and trainers in the lifelong learning sector.* London: LLUK.

Ofsted (2003) *The initial training of further education teachers: A survey.* London: HMI 1762.

Ofsted (2004) *Framework for the Inspection of Initial Training of Further Education Teachers.* London: HMI 2274.

Websites

Ann Gravells – www.anngravells.co.uk

CCEA Northern Ireland – www.rewardinglearning.org.uk

DCELLS Wales – www.wales.gov.uk

Institute for Learning – www.ifl.ac.uk

Learning and Skills Improvement Service – www.lsis.org.uk

Ofqual – www.ofqual.gov.uk

Ofsted – www.ofsted.gov.uk

Qualifications and Credit Framework shortcut – http://tinyurl.com/447bgy2

Scottish Credit and Qualifications Framework – www.scqf.org.uk

Sector Skills Councils – www.sscalliance.org

THE LIFELONG LEARNING SECTOR

Introduction

> In this chapter you will learn about:
> - the Lifelong Learning Sector
> - teaching and learning environments
> - the role of external bodies

The Lifelong Learning Sector

If you are considering becoming a teacher, this could be because you are contemplating a change of career, or feel you have valuable skills and knowledge that you would like to pass on to others. Alternatively, you might be a specialist within your own organisation and train people on the job. Teaching doesn't only happen in schools and colleges, it can take place anywhere, for example, in community centres, prisons and the armed forces. It can also occur in the workplace with apprentices and new or existing staff. You might have shown friends, family and colleagues how to do things and feel you have the ability and skills to be a good teacher, but are not sure yet if you want to take this any further. Perhaps you might currently be teaching but have never been trained how to do it properly. Your own teaching might therefore have been based on how you were originally taught. However, people learn in different ways, some prefer theory and some prefer practice. There are lots of different ways of teaching a subject to help individuals learn. Taking a teacher training qualification will help you to pass on your skills and knowledge to others in a professional and effective way. There are different teaching qualifications which will depend upon the type of teaching role you will have; these are explained in Chapter 2.

Sue Crowley of the Institute for Learning stated:

> *Often new teachers teach as they were taught, then perhaps as they would like to have been taught, and finally they realise different people learn in different ways and a wider spectrum of teaching and learning approaches are needed and available.*

> (*Centres for excellence in teacher training*, 2009: 8)

The Lifelong Learning Sector (LLS) includes teaching and training which can occur in any organisation in the private, public and voluntary sectors. You might be surprised to know that in most instances you do not need to be a qualified or experienced teacher when you start, and you can teach part-time, for example, evening classes, while still working in your current profession. Indeed, it is good practice to maintain your currency of practice in the subject you will teach. What you will need is knowledge of your subject, and passion, enthusiasm and a dedication to helping others learn. There might be particular requirements to teach your subject; for example, if you want to teach welding you might need to be a qualified or experienced welder. You should also have good reading and writing skills and be prepared to use a computer. You can then commence a relevant teaching qualification and learn while you teach.

Teaching can in effect take place any time and anywhere. If someone needs to learn something, then someone else has to teach them to do it. It doesn't always have to lead to a formal qualification at the end of the learning process.

Example

Marie has always been keen on gardening and has worked part-time in a garden centre for the past six years. She feels she has the skills and ability to pass on her knowledge and experience to others. After approaching the local college, she is offered the chance to teach one evening a week. The class does not lead to a qualification, it is a programme aimed at amateur gardeners. The college has asked Marie to enroll on a Preparing to Teach programme to help her plan and manage her sessions.

Teaching is all about helping someone reach their full potential, wherever it might take place. If you choose to teach in the Lifelong Learning Sector, you will have the opportunity to help make a difference to someone's life and career. Teaching can be very rewarding; however, it can also be very demanding. Depending upon where and what you will teach, you might not need to be qualified in your particular subject, but be able to demonstrate appropriate experience and knowledge at a particular level. However, legislation usually requires all new teachers to be working towards an appropriate teaching qualification if they are teaching in further education or on government-funded programmes in England, for example, apprenticeships.

When you start teaching, it could be that you are able to use materials and resources which have been created by someone else. This would be a good start as you will have something to begin with. However, you might need to design all your own materials and handouts. Although this can be very time-consuming it means you are knowledgeable regarding the content of anything you have created. The teaching role involves not only the time you are with your students, but also the preparation time beforehand and the paperwork and marking afterwards.

John Hayes MP, Minister of State for Further Education, Skills and Lifelong Learning stated:

> Opportunities for adults to gain new learning and skills throughout life are the portents of progress and the positive engagement of people with their communities. They are necessary for flexible, innovative and competitive businesses and the jobs they create. They are preconditions of personal growth and social mobility. They are guarantors of the values upon which our democracy is founded.
>
> Working together, colleges, training providers, employers, voluntary organisations and community groups can make an enormous contribution to restoring this country.
>
> (New Challenges, New Chances, 2011: 4)

You can help adult students gain the learning and skills they need to improve their chances both personally and professionally. Teaching isn't just about delivering formally to groups in a classroom; it can take place in many different environments such as the workplace, outdoors or online via the internet. It can also take place at any time, for example during the day, evenings and/or at weekends.

Examples of organisations in the Lifelong Learning Sector include:

- adult education centres
- colleges including specialist and sixth form colleges
- community centres
- companies and organisations
- emergency services
- government-funded training centres
- immigration and detention centres
- prisons and offender centres
- private training organisations
- public services
- probation trusts
- uniformed and armed services
- voluntary organisations

Different organisations will have different expectations of their teachers. For example, if you teach in a college you might have a contract, along with a job description for your teaching role. If you teach in the workplace, you might be training colleagues and, although it might be part of your contract, you might not have a job description which outlines your teaching commitment.

You have probably shown someone how to do something, or explained something to them at some point in your life. If they were able to carry out the task and remember what you told them, then you were successful at teaching them. However, teachers need a lot of patience, and may face many challenges with particular students throughout their career.

Activity

Consider what type of organisation you would like to teach in; for example, a college or private training organisation. If possible, contact those local to you to find out what experience and qualifications you would need to teach. Perhaps you have a lot of experience at work and could train others on the job rather than leaving your current role. If so, find out how you could do this.

Types of student

Students in the Lifelong Learning Sector are aged 14 and above, for example, school groups aged 14–16, college groups aged 16–19 or groups of mixed ages. Each age group will bring with it particular challenges, whether you are teaching a small or large group, or individually on a one-to-one basis. For example, teaching a group of 30 students aged 16–19 in a college would be more challenging than teaching a mature adult individually in the workplace.

14–16 age range

The 14–16 age group are still attending compulsory education. This may bring with it issues that you will have to deal with such as challenging behaviour, truancy, peer pressure, negative attitudes, disruption and bullying. This group will want to be treated as adults but they are still children. You will need to set clear boundaries and establish routines so that a climate of respect and organisation can exist. You will need patience and understanding and must treat everyone in the group as an individual, remaining firm but fair to all. To help maintain respect, it's best not to be on first-name terms, nor to reveal anything personal about yourself.

If you are teaching this age group, you may need to modify the delivery style and methods you would normally use with adults. You might be teaching within the school environment and have to follow their rules and regulations. Conversely the students might come to your organisation and therefore act differently in this environment from the way they normally would at school. They may behave in a more mature manner if given responsibility, or they may act overconfidently and become disruptive in front of their peers.

Ensuring your sessions are meaningful, with lots of interesting and practical tasks, will help classroom control. If you can't use practical tasks, break your session down into lots of smaller aspects, recapping each before moving on. Younger students need lots of praise and encouragement, they appreciate you listening to them and supporting them when necessary. Try and be approachable, and listen to what they have to say. If you ask a student a question and they answer wrongly, don't dismiss their answer, but try and relate it to a real situation which is relevant to the subject. Include all students when asking questions and make them feel their contribution is valued. If you are enthusiastic about the subject, hopefully they will be.

You may need to liaise with relevant school staff on a regular basis. Some students may have learning difficulties; others may come with a support assistant to help them. However, all students will have something positive to contribute to the sessions and you will need to ensure your delivery enables all students to participate in their learning experience.

16–19 age range

The 16–19 age group are not in compulsory education, however some students could be attending a programme as part of an apprenticeship or day-release programme. Non-attendance may affect their funding allowance and you might be required to sign records of attendance to prove they were present. Some problems that you may encounter with the 14–16 age range may also be encountered with the 16–19 age range. For example, if they have to attend as part of a work experience programme and are not attending voluntarily they might not pay as much attention. However, some students may have been (or are still) in employment and will have knowledge and experience that can be drawn on during the sessions. You might therefore have students who have recently left school who are in the same group as students who have been in employment for a while. As a result their levels of maturity will be different. Never assume or underestimate your students' knowledge and draw on this whenever possible.

Young people and adults aged 16 and above

You might be teaching a broad spectrum of ages ranging from 16 upwards, in groups or as individuals. Some students might be apprehensive if they have not attended an educational establishment for a few years. You will therefore need to reassure them that you are there to help them. Depending upon your subject, there will be ways of integrating your students' experiences to benefit everyone.

Example

Haani teaches a weekly two-hour computing programme which will last eight weeks. There are ten students aged 16 to 65. As part of the first session he asks them all to introduce themselves and say a little about their experience of using a computer. He soon realises the older students have very little experience; three have never switched on a computer before. The younger students are more confident and have used computers at school and home. He therefore decides to sit a younger student next to an older one so that they can help and support each other. Each student will be working individually through a series of tasks at their own pace and can ask each other questions rather than calling for help from Haani.

Depending upon your subject, you will find your own ways to reach each individual, giving them confidence to progress with their learning. Always give positive encouragement to retain motivation, and treat all questions as valid, no matter how silly they may seem to you (or the students) at the time.

Workplace students

It could be that you are training apprentices or staff in your place of work. This will usually be on an individual or small group basis. It will give you the opportunity to spend more time with your students if you are in the same environment most days. Hopefully, your staff will be self-motivated and keen to learn and not be disruptive. However, you will have other priorities such as the commitments and deadlines of your own job role to take into consideration. You might be training a student who is with your organisation as part of a work experience programme, they might be with you one day a week, for a full week or more. Even though they might not be in paid employment, you should treat them as a member of staff and make them feel welcome. They might have certain tasks they need to learn and carry out as part of their training programme, you might therefore need to assess their progress and liaise with their teacher.

Distance learning students

Learning is increasingly taking place via a computer outside a formal teaching environment. Programmes can be tailored to individual requirements and students can work at their own pace, at a time and place to suit. If you are teaching online, you might never see or talk to your students, but communicate via the computer program or e-mail. Students need to be self-motivated, committed and able to devote a suitable amount of time to this type of study. Learning can be synchronous, i.e. being online at the same time as their teacher and peers, or asynchronous, i.e. at different times. Some programmes require students to attend a few sessions, and support the rest of their learning through a virtual learning environment (VLE). This is known as *blended learning*, and handouts, activities and resources can be uploaded by the teacher at any time for access by the student. There can still be issues with motivation as students need to be disciplined in aspects such as time management. There could also be issues with behaviour in that some inappropriate comments could be made online. Agreeing a code of conduct from the start could help alleviate this.

Offender students

These students could be in a young offender institution, on remand or in a prison. It might be compulsory that they attend various sessions, and while some will be keen to learn, others may not be. This will bring its own challenges regarding motivation, and there might also be behavioural issues to contend with. If you are teaching in this type of environment you will need to be careful not to allow yourself to become conditioned, or get personal with your students. You will also have strict guidelines to follow. It could be that some of your students are released or moved part way through the programme. Others might start at different points throughout your programme and will need to catch up on what has been taught so far. Some may drop in and out of your sessions due to the prison regime where offenders are attending other activities such as physical education. You might even arrive to teach a session and find that all the prisoners have been locked in their cells due to operational issues. Some might be with visitors or have been moved elsewhere and therefore will not be attending.

Adult students

Adults are usually motivated to learn, either for their own personal benefit or to enhance their job role. This motivation ensures they are keen and enthusiastic students, usually attending voluntarily in their own time, probably in unsociable hours, as they are eager to learn new skills and knowledge.

Adults tend to have a lot of experience, whether it is practical or theoretical, and are often used to being active and having self-discipline when it comes to learning. Adults are more confident to ask questions and challenge theories; they like to relate new learning to their own situations. If you are asked a question you cannot answer, say you will find out, and make sure you do. While you are expected to have an in-depth knowledge of your subject, you won't know everything and it's best to be honest and admit when you don't know something.

Often, adults are not afraid of making a mistake as they have learnt through experience, whereas younger students would not want to embarrass themselves in front of their peers. Adults are often keen to tell you and the group their experiences and how they have learnt from them. Conversely, some adults might lack confidence to discuss things in front of their peers until they get to know them well.

When teaching adults, plan tasks in a logical order, relating theory to practice and involve them with discussions of their own experiences. Always clearly state the aim of your session and how it relates to their learning. Adults need to know the purpose and benefit of any task you ask them to do. Recap and summarise topics, repeat key words and ask questions on an ongoing basis to check that learning is taking place.

Adults will usually make the effort to arrive on time, have the necessary materials, e.g. pens and paper, and not be disruptive. However, you need to consider their personal circumstances and situations, especially if you are delivering an evening class and some of your students have been at work all day.

If a student does arrive a little late, smile and welcome them, give them time to settle down and tell them what you are doing at that moment. You can say you will catch up with them at break time or the end of the session. Try not to make them feel unwelcome or uncomfortable just because they are late. Keep them involved, don't make an example of them or they may decide not to return again.

You could be on first-name terms with adults and have a more informal delivery style (depending upon your subject and your students). Some adults may have had negative experiences at school or of previous programmes they have attended which might have stayed with them, therefore affecting their current learning. Try and get to know each student as an individual to enable you to support their learning in an appropriate way.

Activity

Think back to when you attended school and compare this to a more recent learning experience as an adult. Were your experiences positive or negative? What age group would you like to teach and will your previous experiences of learning influence your teaching styles?

The role of external bodies

There are several external bodies which impact upon education in the Lifelong Learning Sector. These include government departments such as the Department for Education, and stakeholders such as the Skills Funding Agency, who provide the finance for learning to take place. Stakeholders are the organisations who are involved with the regulation, delivery and assessment of accredited qualifications. There are also other organisations which exist to support teaching and learning, for example, professional associations and networking groups. The main external bodies and stakeholders are briefly explained here. However, titles and responsibilities do tend to change, therefore you are advised to check their websites for any updates. Different bodies will exist in the nations of England, Wales, Scotland and Northern Ireland. Website details can be found at the end of the chapter and some will offer you the option to sign up for their electronic newsletters.

Approved centres

These are organisations and companies who deliver, assess and quality assure qualifications accredited through an awarding organisation, for example, colleges, employers and training organisations. Any organisation can apply to become an approved centre to offer qualifications, provided they fulfil certain criteria.

The Association of Colleges

The Association of Colleges (AoC) exists to represent and promote the interests of colleges and to provide members with professional support services. The AoC was established in 1996 by colleges as a voice for further education and higher education. Their membership includes General and Tertiary Further Education Colleges, Sixth Form Colleges and Specialist Colleges in England and Northern Ireland (Wales and Scotland via partnerships).

Centres for Excellence in Teacher Training (CETT)

These are networks which consist of partnerships of organisations involved in initial teacher training (ITT) and continuing professional development (CPD) in the further education system. Their role is to raise the standard of initial teacher education and to improve the quality and consistency of CPD. The centres promote good practice and research, and develop advice and guidance that covers generic teaching issues as well as specific subject resources.

Awarding organisations

Awarding organisations, also known as awarding bodies, provide accreditation for qualifications nationally and internationally. Examples include City and Guilds and Edexcel. They will supply a syllabus or qualification handbook containing guidance regarding the particular qualification to be offered. Inspections will take place by an external verifier, moderator or quality consultant to ensure all requirements are being met. If everything is satisfactory, certificates will be issued to successful students. Any company can become an awarding organisation providing they fulfil the necessary Ofqual criteria.

Council for the Curriculum, Examinations and Assessment (CCEA) (Northern Ireland)

The CCEA is a non-departmental public body reporting to the Department of Education in Northern Ireland. They advise the government regarding what should be taught in Northern Ireland's schools and colleges. They monitor standards to ensure that the qualifications and examinations offered by awarding bodies in Northern Ireland are of an appropriate quality and standard, and they also award qualifications.

Department for Business, Innovation and Skills (BIS)

BIS brings all aspects of the economy together, for example, business and trade, higher education, innovation, science and skills in the United Kingdom. They are committed to fostering competitive markets through business law frameworks, enabling companies to compete freely and giving consumers choice and value. They are also responsible for consumer law, employment matters and enterprise and business support.

They are creating a high-quality and responsive further education sector that equips workers with the skills demanded in a modern globalised economy. They are also committed to fostering world-class higher education to provide the nation with the high-level skills needed for economic success, while ensuring excellence in teaching and research.

Department for Children, Education, Lifelong Learning and Skills (DCELLS) (Wales)

DCELLS is an executive body of the Welsh Assembly Government. They aim to promote high expectations and performance for all students with effective regulation, inspection and support. They fund and develop post-16 provision (apart from Higher Education) throughout Wales by targeting low, intermediate and high skill levels to enable more individuals, communities and employers to succeed in Wales.

Department for Education (DfE)

The DfE is a government department responsible for education and children's services in schools in England. This includes issues affecting young people up to the age of 19 and includes child protection and education. They are committed to cutting unnecessary burdens and to giving teachers the freedom and autonomy they need to get on with their jobs. Part of this is making it easier for teachers to understand how to fulfil their legal obligations and exercise their statutory powers by making guidance and advisory content clearer and more succinct.

Learning and Skills Improvement Service (LSIS)

LSIS is the Lifelong Learning Sector Skills Council that aims to accelerate the drive for excellence in the learning and skills sector in England. They build on the sector's own capacity to design, commission and deliver improvement and strategic change. They are currently the holder of the professional teaching standards, having taken over from Lifelong Learning UK (LLUK) in 2011. They have a resource website called *Excellence Gateway* which you might like to look at for your particular subject area.

National Apprenticeship Service (NAS)

The NAS is responsible for apprenticeships in England and was designed to increase the number of opportunities for both employers and students. They are simplifying the process of recruiting an apprentice through an online web-based matching service. Apprenticeships bring considerable value to organisations, employers, individuals and the economy. They are a great way of training, developing and skilling young people for the future. They help businesses secure a supply of people with the skills and qualities they need.

Office for Standards in Education, Children's Services and Skills (Ofsted)

Ofsted inspects and regulates services in England which care for children and young people, and those providing education and skills for students of all ages. They were originally established to inspect schools; however, they now inspect provision in the Lifelong Learning Sector, including teacher training, according to a common inspection framework. Ofsted reports directly to Parliament and is independent and impartial. Inspections of organisations are carried out and the results are published on their website. The aim of inspections is to promote improvement and value for money in the services inspected and regulated, so that children and young people, parents and carers, adult students and employers all benefit.

Office of Qualifications and Examinations Regulation (Ofqual)

Ofqual is the regulator of qualifications, examinations and assessments in England and vocational qualifications in Northern Ireland. They are not directly controlled by the government but report to Parliament. They are responsible for maintaining standards, improving confidence in the system and distributing information about qualifications. Ofqual give formal recognition to awarding organisations and bodies that deliver and award qualifications. They also monitor their qualifications and activities, including the fees charged.

Professional bodies, associations and networks

Professional bodies exist to support their members in a particular area, for example, teaching and assessing. A few are detailed here in alphabetical order, and their website details can be found at the end of the chapter.

Chartered Institute of Educational Assessors (CIEA)

The CIEA is a professional body dedicated to supporting the needs of everyone involved in educational assessment. This includes senior examiners, moderators and markers, as well as individuals with an interest in or responsibility for assessment in primary schools, secondary schools, colleges, universities, training centres and other educational organisations. Membership is open to everyone with an interest in educational assessment as well as those studying to become teachers.

General Teaching Council (GTC)

The GTC is the professional body for teaching in England; there is a separate one for Scotland. Their purpose is to help improve standards of teaching and learning in schools and they are open to teachers, employers and parents.

Institute for Learning (IfL)

The IfL is the professional body for teachers, tutors, trainers and student teachers in the Lifelong Learning Sector. All teachers and trainers working in publicly funded further education and skills provision in England are required to register as members of IfL, undertake continuing professional development (CPD) every year and abide by their Code of Professional Practice (2009). The IfL also has a social network facility which all members are free to join. Please see Chapter 4 for further details of the IfL.

National Institute of Adult Continuing Education (NIACE)

NIACE aims to encourage all adults to engage in learning of all kinds. They are the largest adult learning non-government organisation in the world, and a lead advocacy body in England and Wales with direct contact with policymakers. Anyone can become a member and play a role in the governance of the institute and influence strategic direction. NIACE operates across all post-compulsory education and training sectors, and works with other agencies to secure the interests of all adult students.

Post Compulsory Education and Training (PCET)

PCET is a free UK-based networking site for teachers. It has a dedicated website which has been designed to support further education teachers from all subject areas. The PCET website will provide you with a place to share advice, resources and knowledge with your peers.

Social networking sites

There are many social networking sites and most are free to join; however, not all are appropriate for professional teachers. With all social network sites, you need to be careful what you say as your words will instantly be in the public domain. You also need to be careful of the information you are sharing and ensure your profile only includes the details you are happy to share with anyone. Nevertheless, joining certain social networking sites can prove beneficial.

Sector Skills Councils and Standard Setting Bodies (SSC/SSB)

These are employer-led organisations which gather information and labour market intelligence to influence the development of qualifications and apprenticeships. Each SSC represents an area of business or industry, and which there will be one for the subject you will teach, for example, construction, finance, hospitality and information technology. For some subjects they are known as Standard Setting Bodies (SSB). All SSCs are members of the Alliance of Sector Skills Councils and are recognised by government throughout the United Kingdom (UK) as the independent, employer-led organisations which ensure that the skills system is driven by employers' needs. As a result, they have a major impact on the delivery of publicly and privately funded training throughout the UK. The Learning and Skills Improvement Service (LSIS) is the Sector Skills Council for the teacher training standards. SSCs produce the national occupational standards (NOS) which awarding organisations can then turn into qualifications. They also state how the qualifications should be assessed by producing an assessment strategy or assessment guidance.

Skills Funding Agency (SfA)

The SfA is a partner of the Department for Business, Innovation and Skills (BIS). Their role is to fund adult further education and skills training in England. They ensure that people and businesses can access the skills training they need to succeed in playing their part in society and in growing England's economy. They invest approximately £4 billion per year in colleges and training organisations to fund training for adults in England. The skills training they fund enables people to do their jobs better, get new jobs, or progress in their careers. The SfA is also responsible for the National Apprenticeship Service (NAS) and champions high standards of training and development through the running of various vocational skills competitions and awards.

Example

Abdul recently achieved his PTLLS Award and joined the Institute for Learning (IfL). He noticed the IfL had a members' online community which he could join via their website www.ifl.ac.uk. He was able to network with other teachers and discuss aspects relating to becoming fully qualified. He also joined LinkedIn® at www.linkedin.co.uk, a professional networking service. Becoming a member entitled him to join established groups, enabling him to network with others in his subject area. He was able to discuss relevant topics and keep up to date with developments in his area.

Universities Council for the Education of Teachers (UCET)

UCET acts as a national forum for the discussion of matters which relate to the education of teachers and professional educators, and to the study of education in the university sector. It contributes to the formulation of policy in these fields. Members are universities in the United Kingdom which are involved in teacher education plus a number of colleges of higher education in the university sector.

Unions

There are several unions that you might be eligible to join depending upon where you teach and the age range of your students. These include the Association of Teachers and Lecturers (ATL), the National Union of Teachers (NUT), the National Association of Schoolmasters Union of Women Teachers (NASUWT) and the University and College Union (UCU). You can also join the National Union of Students (NUS) if you are working towards a qualification. Unions aim to support their members, give advice and guidance and often offer discounted products and services.

Young people's learning agency (YPLA)

The YPLA is sponsored by the Department for Education and exists to support the funding of training and education for all 16–19-year-olds in England. The YPLA was launched in April 2010 with the mission of championing education and training for young people in England. They do this by providing financial support to young learners, funding Academies and supporting local authorities to commission suitable education and training opportunities for all 16–19-year-olds. Subject to the passage of legislation, the Education Funding Agency (part of the Department for Education) will take over responsibility from the YPLA on 1 April 2012 for the funding of young people's education and training, including the increasing number of Academies. From April 2012, a Youth Contract provides a minimum of 410,000 new work places for 18–24 year olds.

Activity

Research the external bodies, stakeholders, organisations and groups that are involved with the teaching and support of your subject. Look at their websites and register for their electronic updates if available. You could also become a member of any relevant organisations which interest you.

Summary

In this chapter you have learnt about:

- the Lifelong Learning Sector
- teaching and learning environments
- the role of external bodies

Theory focus

References and further information

Dennick, R and Exley, K (2004) *Small Group Teaching: Tutorials, Seminars and Beyond*. Abingdon: Routledge.

Department for Business, Innovation and Skills (2011) *New Challenges, New Chances: next steps in implementing the further education reform programme*. London: BIS.

IfL (2009) *Code of Professional Practice: Raising concerns about IfL members (V2)*. London: Institute for Learning.

Illeris, K (2010) *The Fundamentals of Workplace Learning: Understanding How People Learn in Working Life*. Abingdon: Routledge.

Kidd, W and Czerniawski, G (2010) *Successful Teaching 14–19*. London: Sage Publications Ltd.

Knowles *et al.* (2011) *The Adult Learner* (7th edition) Abingdon: Routledge.

LLUK (2006) *New overarching professional standards for teachers, tutors and trainers in the Lifelong Learning Sector*. London: LLUK.

LSIS (2009) *Centres for excellence in teacher training: CETT Standard*. Learning and Skills Improvement Service Newsletter issue 1.

Peart, S and Atkins, L (2011) *Teaching 14–19 Learners in the Lifelong Learning Sector*. Exeter: Learning Matters.

Powell, S and Tummons, J (2011) *Inclusive Practice in the Lifelong Learning Sector*. Exeter: Learning Matters.

Rogers, A and Horrocks, N (2010) *Teaching Adults* (4th edition). Maidenhead: Open University Press.

Websites

Alliance of Sector Skills Councils – www.sscalliance.org

Association of Teachers and Lecturers – www.atl.org.uk

Centres for Excellence in Teacher Training (CETT) –
http://cett.excellencegateway.org.uk/

CIEA – www.ciea.org.uk

City and Guilds – www.cityandguilds.com

Council for the Curriculum, Examinations and Assessment (Northern Ireland)
– www.rewardinglearning.org.uk

Department for Business, Innovation and Skills – www.bis.gov.uk

Department for Children, Education, Lifelong Learning and Skills (Wales) –
http://wales.gov.uk/topics/educationandskills/?lang=en

Department for Education – www.education.gov.uk

Edexcel – www.edexcel.com

Excellence Gateway – www.excellencegateway.org

General Teaching Council for England – www.gtce.org.uk

General Teaching Council for Scotland – www.gtcs.org.uk

Institute for Learning – www.ifl.ac.uk

Learning and Skills Improvement Service – www.lsis.org.uk

LinkedIn® professional networking services – www.linkedin.co.uk

National Apprenticeship Service – www.apprenticeships.org.uk

National Association of Schoolmasters Union of Women Teachers –
www.nasuwt.org.uk

National Union of Students – www.nus.org.uk

National Union of Teachers – www.teachers.org.uk

NIACE – www.niace.org.uk

Office for Standards in Education, Children's Services and Skills –
www.ofsted.gov.uk

Office of Qualifications and Examinations Regulation – www.ofqual.gov.uk

Sector Skills Council – www.sscalliance.org

Skills Funding Agency – www.skillsfundingagency.bis.gov.uk.

Universities Council for the Education of Teachers – www.ucet.ac.uk

University and College Union – www.ucu.org.uk

Young People's Learning Agency – www.ypla.gov.uk

Youth Contract – http://dwp.gov.uk/youth-contract

Introduction

In this chapter you will learn about:
- choosing a subject or qualification to teach
- getting qualified
- obtaining a teaching position

Choosing a subject or qualification to teach

Teachers in schools are often expected to teach several different subjects after achieving a degree and attending full-time teacher training. However, in the Lifelong Learning Sector, teaching is often based on the experience, knowledge and skills gained from a profession, hobby or interest rather than a degree. The specialist subject you choose to teach will probably be based on your current or previous job, whether you are qualified or not. Qualifications in your subject can always be achieved later if they are a requirement. For example, you might wish to teach an evening pottery class which does not require you to hold a pottery qualification; you might just be required to be a skilled potter. Conversely, you might wish to teach motor vehicle maintenance and, to do this, you will need to hold a motor vehicle maintenance qualification.

Most classes in the Lifelong Learning Sector are vocational, in other words, aimed at people who wish to gain skills in a particular trade or skill. However, there are also classes which are academic, in other words, for people who wish to gain knowledge, for example, English literature.

First of all, you need to think about what your subject specialism could be. You might have taken a higher level qualification many years ago and feel you would like to teach it, for example, history. Your career for many years might not have utilised your history knowledge and therefore you feel a little out of date. There's no reason why you couldn't take a refresher programme to ensure you are current with your historical knowledge. You can always change your mind regarding your subject; for example, if you start the Award in Preparing to Teach in the Lifelong Learning Sector (PTLLS), planning to teach history, but don't enjoy your micro teaching session, you can always rethink. You will need to find out what the requirements are to teach your subject of choice and what qualifications and experience you would need. You might not need to have them when you start teaching and quite often you can gain them while you are teaching.

Example

Richard has been an amateur photographer for many years and has a lot of experience of traditional and digital photography. However, he has never achieved any photographic qualifications. His full-time occupation is a librarian and he would like to continue this, while teaching evening classes in photography. He has decided to take a Level 3 Certificate in Photo Imaging part-time at his local college. He has also applied to take the PTLLS Award while he is there. He hopes to make some contacts at the college which might lead to a part-time teaching job.

If you are planning to teach in the workplace, for example, training new staff or apprentices on the job, you might not need any qualifications, just experience and knowledge that you can effectively pass on.

If you do become a qualified teacher in a particular subject specialism, you will be classed as a *dual professional*. This means you are a professional teacher as well as a professional in your specialist subject.

You could always contact your local college or training organisation to ask if you could observe a teaching session in your subject area. This will help you see what is involved in being a teacher. You would make some useful contacts and you could ask what the requirements are to teach your chosen subject.

Accredited qualifications and non-accredited programmes

Accredited qualifications are those which lead to a recognised certificate, for example, a Certificate in Hospitality. Certificates will be issued through an awarding organisation after their syllabus has been delivered, assessed and quality assured. If you wish to teach on programmes which lead to accredited qualifications you will need to fulfil the requirements of the awarding organisation. They will state what qualifications and/or experience you need to teach the subject. This is known as an *assessment strategy* and you can find this out by looking in the syllabus, usually under the human resources section. It is possible to start teaching accredited programmes without holding a teaching certificate, providing you begin working towards the PTLLS Award within six months of commencing your teaching role. Most accredited qualifications are on the Qualifications and Credit Framework (QCF) and are called Awards, Certificates and Diplomas depending upon how long they take to achieve. Further information regarding the QCF can be found in the Introduction (pages 1–9).

Non-accredited programmes are those which do not lead to a recognised certificate, for example, cake decorating. However, students might be issued with a record of attendance, a record of achievement, or a certificate of competence by the organisation who offered the programme. These certificates do not hold any value professionally, but are recognition of personal achievement. There might not be a syllabus for the subject, therefore you would need to devise the content of the programme yourself. You may not need to be qualified in the subject area, just experienced and knowledgeable. If you are going to teach on programmes which do not receive government funding, you might not even need a teaching qualification.

Activity

Think of a subject you could teach. This might be something related to your current or previous job, or a hobby or interest. What experience, knowledge, skills and qualifications do you already have? What further training and/or qualifications do you think you may need to teach this subject? You could contact your local college to find out what the requirements are to teach your chosen subject.

Getting qualified

There are several ways in which you can become a qualified teacher. You could take a part-time programme, for example, a daytime or evening class while you are still working in your current profession (known as *pre-service*). Instead of part-time, you could attend a full-time teacher training programme, although these are usually for graduates. Alternatively, you could take a teacher training programme while you are also teaching your chosen subject (known as *in-service*). There are other forms of attendance, for example, day release, blocks of learning, perhaps a week or more at a time, and distance learning. Teachers need to have practical experience of teaching their subject while they are learning to demonstrate putting theory into practice. You would therefore need to deliver a certain amount of teaching practice hours while taking the programme.

The Lifelong Learning Sector qualifications are made up of units which can be taken separately or together depending upon where you choose to study. The length of time taken will also vary; some organisations offer very intensive training programmes, whereas others take longer. Wherever you choose to study, the content of the qualification should be the same. If it's a requirement that you achieve a teaching qualification, you will have five years within which to become fully qualified. This does not mean the training lasts for five years, it might only take one or two on a part-time basis. It just means you have five years from when you start teaching to becoming qualified.

Once you have decided you are going to gain a teaching qualification you need to contact your local college or training provider. They will tell you what teaching qualifications are on offer and what the attendance requirements are. While you are working towards your teaching qualifications, it would be extremely useful to have a *mentor*, someone who can help and support you, not only with teaching skills, but also with your chosen specialist subject. Choosing the right mentor is important as you will want someone you can get along with and feel you can go to for support.

Lifelong Learning professional teaching standards

In September 2007, standards came into effect for all new teachers in the Lifelong Learning Sector who teach or assess on government-funded programmes in England. This includes all post-16 education, including Further Education, Adult and Community Learning, Work-based Learning and Offender Education. Please see the web links at the end of the chapter for Northern Ireland, Scotland and Wales.

The teaching standards identified what teachers should know and be able to do and are divided into six *domains*:

A Professional Values and Practice
B Learning and Teaching
C Specialist Learning and Teaching
D Planning for Learning
E Assessment for Learning
F Access and Progression

Awarding organisations incorporate the standards into qualifications, all of which start with the *Award in Preparing to Teach in the Lifelong Learning Sector* (PTLLS). If you are aiming to become fully qualified, you should cover all aspects of the six domains throughout your teaching role while working towards the relevant qualification.

Teaching qualifications

All new teachers should undertake the Award in Preparing to Teach in the Lifelong Learning Sector (PTLLS) at the beginning of their career. This can be as a discrete Award or embedded in the Certificate (CTLLS) or Diploma

(DTLLS) in Teaching in the Lifelong Learning Sector qualifications. Higher education institutions still use the term *Certificate in Education (Cert Ed)* even though the content is the same as the Diploma. There is also a *Professional Graduate Certificate in Education* and a *Postgraduate Certificate in Education (PGCE)*, which again cover the same content as DTLLS but are offered at higher levels.

CTLLS is for *associate teachers*, who usually teach from materials prepared by others. DTLLS or the equivalent is for *full teachers*, who have more responsibility for designing materials and resources for teaching and assessing. Full teachers will teach individuals and groups at different levels. Chapter 4 covers the associate and full teacher roles in more detail.

There are other programmes which you could take, for example, *Train the Trainer* programmes. However, these are not recognised as teaching qualifications but they will give you the basic skills and knowledge required to begin teaching.

Award in Preparing to Teach in the Lifelong Learning Sector (PTLLS)

The PTLLS Award is the first step towards achieving the Certificate or Diploma. It is usually a short programme consisting of the basics of teaching and learning. You do not need to be in a teaching role and the Award is ideal if you just want to find out what it's like to teach without becoming a teacher. If you take the Award you will be required to deliver a short session to your peers if you are pre-service, or to your current students if you are in-service, known as micro-teaching.

The PTLLS Award is made up of the following four units or their *accepted alternatives*.

- Roles, Responsibilities and Relationships in Lifelong Learning
- Understanding Inclusive Learning and Teaching in Lifelong Learning
- Using Inclusive Learning and Teaching Approaches in Lifelong Learning
- Principles of Assessment in Lifelong Learning.

The PTLLS Award is 12 credits on the QCF; this means a total of 120 hours must be dedicated to achieve the qualification. This time will be a mixture of contact time with a teacher/assessor and non-contact time for self-study.

The PTLLS Award is offered at two levels to differentiate for student abilities. The content is the same at both level 3 and level 4; the difference in level is expressed through the skills and knowledge required for achievement. For example, if you are taking level 3 you will *explain* how or why you do something, at level 4 you will *analyse* how or why you do it. If you are working towards level 4 you will need to carry out relevant research and use an academic style of writing and reference your work to relevant textbooks.

Accepted alternatives come from the Learning and Development qualifications. However, there are rules as to which ones can be used, known as *rules of combination*.

The accepted alternative units are:

- Facilitate learning and development for individuals (level 3, 6 credits)
- Facilitate learning and development in groups (level 3, 6 credits)
- Manage learning and development in groups (level 4, 6 credits)
- Understanding the principles and practices of assessment (level 3, 3 credits)

Example

Jodi had been working as an assessor in her place of work and had achieved the QCF unit called Understanding the Principles and Practices of Assessment. She achieved this as part of the Award in Assessing Competence in the Work Environment. She then began teaching and wanted to take the PTLLS Award. She was therefore exempt from the Principles of Assessment in Lifelong Learning unit as she had an equivalent QCF unit.

Certificate in teaching in the Lifelong Learning Sector (CTLLS)

The Certificate contains the four units from the PTLLS Award, plus other units, some mandatory and some optional, and is 36 credits on the QCF. This means a total of 360 hours must be dedicated to achieve the qualification. This time will be a mixture of contact time with a teacher/assessor and non-contact time for self-study. CTLLS is the qualification for associate teachers, i.e. those with less responsibility than full teachers. It is offered at level 3 and level 4 and 30 teaching practice hours are required, therefore you do need to be teaching to take this qualification. You will be observed in your teaching environment for approximately three hours.

Diploma in teaching in the Lifelong Learning Sector (DTLLS)

The Diploma contains the four units from the PTLLS Award, plus mandatory and optional units, and is 120 credits on the QCF. This means a total of 1,200 hours must be dedicated to achieve the qualification. This time will be a mixture of contact time with a teacher/assessor and non-contact time for self-study. You will need to demonstrate 100 teaching practice hours with students, therefore you do need to be teaching to achieve this qualification. You will be observed in your teaching environment for approximately eight hours.

What do the teaching qualifications include?

The teaching qualifications will usually cover the following aspects; however, the depth at which you will learn will differ depending upon which qualification you take and the level at which you will achieve it.

- Teaching roles, responsibilities, administration and record keeping.
- Planning to teach, i.e. preparing a scheme of work, session plans and teaching and learning materials and resources.
- Teaching approaches, i.e. using different methods and strategies for different subjects and students, how to manage groups and individuals and how students learn.
- Theories of teaching and learning.
- Assessing, i.e. preparing and using assessment activities, marking and giving feedback.
- Quality assurance, i.e. evaluating the teaching and learning process and reflecting upon own practice.

Besides learning the above, you need to have qualities and skills that will help you convey your subject to your students, for example, passion, enthusiasm and dedication. As part of the Institute for Learning's strategic aim to promote the professional status of teachers and trainers, it collaborated with national organisations representing students to develop a model of the ideal teacher and trainer. The qualities required include:

- *Knowledge – of both the subject and the student. The experience of learning providers is of real importance to students. This applied not only to teaching practice but also to keeping up to date with their field of expertise.*
- *Professionalism – well-presented and appropriate for a person of authority. Students felt that the status of their learning providers was of real importance. This was expressed through a range of attributes from personal appearance through to a flexible approach and time management skills.*
- *Communication and support – present their lesson skilfully and engagingly. Creativity and enthusiasm are attributes in a teacher that are valued highly by students. Passion for the subject seems to be contagious and a creative and innovative approach to teaching is really appreciated.*
  (http://www.ifl.ac.uk/old-landing-pages/ifl-community/learner-voice, accessed 24 November 2011)

Assessment qualifications

There are qualifications available for assessors who make decisions as to progress and achievement, for example, those who assess apprentices in their place of work. The apprentice might be trained by their workplace supervisor, but assessed by someone else who is a specialist in the subject area as well as a specialist assessor (i.e. a dual professional).

If you are assessing qualifications which are classed as National Vocational Qualifications (NVQs) it is mandatory that you achieve an Assessor Award within a given time period, usually 18 months.

The assessor qualifications contain three units at level 3; the first is knowledge based and the other two are performance based. As the first unit is purely knowledge based, it can be taken prior to, or at the same time as, the performance unit. It is ideal for anyone who wants to know what it's like to be an assessor but who does not have anyone to assess. The units can be achieved in any order and each has a credit value on the Qualifications and Credit Framework (QCF). The first unit is accepted towards achievement of the PTLLS Award.

1. Understanding the principles and practices of assessment (3 credits).
   This is a knowledge-based unit for new and existing assessors or anyone who wishes to know about the theory of assessment. You do not need to carry out any assessment activities with students to achieve this unit.
2. Assess occupational competence in the work environment (6 credits).
   This is a performance unit for anyone who assesses in the work environment using methods such as observations, questions and examining products of work. The assessments might be towards a qualification, or to confirm an employee's workplace competence towards their job specification.
3. Assess vocational skills, knowledge and understanding (6 credits).
   This is a performance unit for anyone who assesses in any environment using methods such as assignments, projects, simulations and tests. The assessments might be towards qualifications or programmes of learning.

Units 1 and 2 will lead to the *Award in Assessing Competence in the Work Environment*; units 1 and 3 will lead to the *Award in Assessing Vocationally Related Achievement*. If all three units are achieved this will lead to the *Certificate in Assessing Vocational Achievement*.

Internal quality assurance qualifications

There are three units at level 4; the first is knowledge based and the other two are performance based. As the first unit is purely knowledge based, it can be taken prior to, or at the same time, as the performance unit. It is ideal for anyone who wants to know what it's like to be an internal quality assurer but who does not yet have anything to quality assure. The units can be achieved in any order and each has a credit value on the QCF.

1. Understanding the principles and practices of internally assuring the quality of assessment (6 credits).

    This is a knowledge-based unit for new and existing internal quality assurers or anyone who wishes to know about the theory of internal quality assurance. You do not need to carry out any internal quality assurance activities with assessors to achieve this unit.

2. Internally assure the quality of assessment (6 credits).

    This is a performance unit for anyone who internally quality assures the work of assessors; for example, observing practice, sampling judgements and decisions, supporting and advising assessors. It can be achieved in any environment by internally quality assuring qualifications, programmes of learning or workplace competence.

3. Plan, allocate and monitor work in own area of responsibility (5 credits).

    This is a performance unit for anyone who leads the internal quality assurance process within an organisation. The role will include having a responsibility for managing the quality and performance of assessors and/or other internal quality assurers. Developing systems and liaising with external inspectors might also be part of this role.

Units 1 and 2 will lead to the *Award in internally assuring the quality of assessment*; Units 1, 2 and 3 will lead to the *Certificate in leading the internal quality assurance of assessment processes and practice*.

Learning and Development Qualifications

The assessment and quality assurance units form part of the Learning and Development Qualifications and as a whole they are known as *TAQA – Training, Assessment and Quality Assurance*. These qualifications are more suited for those who train and assess in the workplace. Some units can be used towards the teaching qualifications; however, the full Learning and Development qualification is not acceptable as a substitute for them.

These qualifications consist of units which cover knowledge and practice, just like the teaching qualifications, and are available at levels 3 and 4. If you wish to achieve the Learning and Development qualifications, you cannot use them to apply for your Licence to Practise as a teacher.

Funding for qualifications

It may be possible to obtain funding to help you achieve a recognised teaching qualification. There might be grants, loans and bursaries available, particularly in certain skill shortage areas such as construction, maths and science. However, you will need to check this through the organisation where you would like to teach. Sometimes, the organisation will pay for your qualifications, providing you remain with them for an agreed period of time. If you leave before this time is up, you might have to repay the costs.

Activity

Find out more about the teaching qualifications you feel would be appropriate for you. This could be by contacting local colleges or training organisations, or searching the internet. Find out how you could enroll, how much they will cost, and if any funding is available.

Obtaining a teaching position

It can be overwhelming making a career move from your current profession into teaching, or indeed continuing working while teaching as a dual professional. Once you have made the decision that you would like to teach, you need to research what teaching positions are available for the amount of time you are able to commit. For example, you might like to give up your current career and teach full-time, or you might like to teach evening classes while continuing working. Teaching positions in the Lifelong Learning Sector will differ depending upon the demand for your particular subject. You could be:

● full-time (permanent or termly contract)

● part-time (permanent or temporary contract)

● peripatetic (working for several organisations)

● self-employed (invoicing for work done, without the benefits of being an employee)

● sessional (hourly paid)

● supply (providing temporary cover for absent staff through an agency)

● voluntary (unpaid)

The type of contract you receive will depend upon your employer. However, your entitlement to sick pay, holiday pay and access to a pension scheme will depend upon whether you are employed via an agency or directly with the organisation. If you are self-employed you will need to invoice for any work you carry out and will need relevant insurance policies. If you are a part-time, peripatetic, sessional or supply teacher, you will need to complete a pay claim, usually on a monthly basis.

If you are a full-time teacher, you will be allocated a certain number of teaching hours per week (known as *contact time*) with your students. The rest of the time is for preparation, marking, attending meetings, etc. You will need to be prepared to put in time of your own, particularly if you are part-time or sessional. Even though you might feel you get a good hourly rate of pay for teaching, you have to take into account that this covers you for all the work you do which is outside of these hours. Most organisations in the Lifelong Learning Sector work throughout the year, therefore don't expect to have long breaks as school teachers do.

Rates of pay will vary depending upon your job role, where you teach and what subject and level you will teach. If you teach a degree programme, you are likely to receive a higher rate of pay than if you teach a lower level programme. This does not mean it's harder to teach a degree; teaching can be very time-consuming and challenging whatever is being taught at whatever level. However, you may have more responsibility and be recognised for the higher level qualifications you have personally achieved. For example, you usually need a Master's degree in your subject specialism before you can teach a degree programme.

Teaching positions might be called something other than *teacher* depending upon what will be taught and where, for example:

- assessor
- coach
- counsellor
- facilitator
- instructor
- lecturer
- mentor
- presenter
- supervisor
- trainer
- tutor

Sometimes, rates of pay are determined by titles, for example, a lecturer might receive more than an instructor.

Applying for a teaching position

Once you have decided on a subject you would like to teach, you need to approach suitable organisations that require teachers. Don't worry if you are not a qualified teacher at this point, as long as you are willing to work towards a teaching qualification it should not affect the application process.

You could find out what colleges, training organisations, adult education centres etc. there are in your area and politely contact them to ask if they have any teaching positions available. If they do, ask for an application form. If they don't, ask if you can send them your curriculum vitae for them to keep on file. Don't be put off by rejection, you need to persevere and stay positive.

Curriculum vitae

A curriculum vitae (CV) is a document containing details about you, your experience and your qualifications which are relevant to the job role you are applying for. It's useful to keep your CV up to date so that it's ready should a position arise which you would like to apply for. There is no requirement for you to include details such as marital status, number of children or your date of birth as these should not affect an interviewer's decision. However, you might need to give further details on an application form or at interview if required.

Your CV can take many formats, it's best to keep it simple and to the point, don't use jargon and keep it to two sides of A4 paper or less. Information should always be tailored to the position you are applying for and can include:

- name and contact details
- personal statement – your strengths and achievements in particular areas
- experience – what you have done which relates to the position you are applying for
- education and qualifications – what you have studied and achieved
- career history – your current and previous job title and responsibilities (most recent first)
- interests – useful if you have hobbies which relate to the position you are applying for
- references – details of two people who could be contacted (always check with them first)

If you are sending your CV to organisations, whether this is in response to an advertisement or just speculation, it's best to write a covering letter to go with it. This should state why you would like to work for the particular organisation, what your specialist subject is and whether you would like to work full-time or part-time. It could also state other skills you have, for example, if you feel you are capable of teaching several different subjects. Your letter and CV should be word processed and checked for spelling, grammar and punctuation errors. You don't want to give a bad impression before you even start.

Remember to make sure your letter and CV look professional and include your contact details.

The government website https://nextstep.direct.gov.uk has lots of advice regarding creating a CV, writing covering letters and applying for jobs.

Preparing for an interview

You should have received a *job description* or *person specification* when you applied for the teaching position. These will usually state the requirements of the job role, i.e. responsibilities, duties and conditions of employment. Often, the requirements are listed as *essential* or *desirable*.

Example

Essential
Hold the Level 3 Health and Social Care Diploma or equivalent
Hold a recognised teaching qualification or be willing to work towards DTLLS
Have good literacy and ICT skills
Have the ability to work independently

Desirable
Have good numeracy skills
Have a clean driving licence
Hold an assessor qualification
Have experience of working in a Health and Social Care setting

If you meet all the essential requirements, you should be in with a good chance of getting an interview, depending upon who else has applied. If you meet most of the desirable requirements, you might be able to discuss those you do not meet. For example, if you have three points on your driving licence it might not go against you. Most teaching positions require you to undertake a Criminal Records Bureau (CRB) check, particularly if you are working with under 18-year-olds or vulnerable adults. If you have a criminal record, it's best to disclose this before the CRB check is carried out. It could be that what shows on your record is not relevant to the position you have applied for.

Consider how long it will take you to get to the venue, what transport arrangements you need to make or what parking facilities are available. Make sure you plan what you are going to wear and how you will act, i.e. your body language and communication skills.

Make sure you research the organisation you hope to work for before your interview, you can usually find out all about them via their website if they have one. Having prior knowledge of the organisation can help when answering questions, and give you ideas of some questions to ask. Think of questions that you might be asked, and consider your responses, for example, *Why do you want to work for this organisation?* and *What are your strengths?* Think of some questions you could ask, for example, *What opportunities are there for staff training and development?* If you are asked questions you don't know the answer to, just be honest, or say *That's a really good question, I hadn't considered that, but I will now.* Never bluff your way or make up an answer. Being honest should help you gain respect. Make sure you take everything you need with you, for example, original certificates, evidence of achievements, proof you are entitled to work in this country and your CV. Planning in advance will save you becoming stressed or anxious on the day.

You might be asked beforehand to deliver a short presentation as part of the interview process and this could be in front of the interview panel or a small group of students. Make sure you fully address the topic you have been given and practise it at home, checking your content and timings carefully. Ask in advance if you are required to use presentation equipment and, if so, what will be available. For example, if you are preparing a computerised presentation, ask which version of the software you should use. You might need to e-mail the presentation in advance, or take it on a memory stick. When you present your topic, be passionate about your subject, use eye contact with everyone and portray confidence through your voice projection and body language.

At the end of your interview, you should be told when you can expect to hear if you have got the position. If you do get it, make sure you find out what you are expected to do and when. If you don't get it, ask for feedback as to how you could improve for future interviews. Never be demoralised, it might take several interviews before you are offered a suitable position.

Activity

Read the local newspaper, visit a job or careers centre and search the internet for teaching positions in your specialist subject area. Some websites are listed at the end of the chapter and you will be able to sign up for regular alerts. Some jobs can also be located via groups on professional social networking sites such as LinkedIn® (www.linkedin.co.uk). If you see a job that interests you, obtain further information and apply for it if you feel you could do it.

Summary

In this chapter you have learnt about:

- choosing a subject or qualification to teach
- getting qualified
- obtaining a teaching position

Theory focus

References and further information

Further Education Teachers' Qualifications (England) Regulations (2007) – www.legislation.gov.uk/uksi/2007/2264/contents/made

Further Education Teachers' Qualifications (Wales) – http://tiny.cc/o8who

Gravells, A (2012) *Achieving your TAQA Assessor and Internal Quality Assurer Award*. Exeter: Learning Matters.

Gravells, A (2012) *Preparing to Teach in the Lifelong Learning Sector: The New Award* (5th edition). Exeter: Learning Matters.

Learning and Skills Improvement Service – www.lsis.org.uk

LLUK (2006) *New overarching professional standards for teachers, tutors and trainers in the Lifelong Learning Sector*. London: Skills for Business.

Professional Standards for Lecturers in Scotland – http://tiny.cc/3w9jg

Professional Standards for Teachers, Tutors and Trainers in the Lifelong Learning Sector – http://tinyurl.com/4xkcz5z

Teaching Qualifications for Northern Ireland – http://tiny.cc/2bexb

Websites

Creating a curriculum vitae – https://nextstep.direct.gov.uk/gettingajob

Criminal Records Bureau – www.crb.gov.uk

Employment support – www.direct.gov.uk/en/Employment/index.htm

Teaching grants and bursaries – www.ifl.ac.uk/membership/initial-teacher-training-itt

Teaching positions in the Lifelong Learning Sector:
www.eatjobs.co.uk
www.fecareers.co.uk
www.fejobs.com
www.jobs.ac.uk
www.tes.co.uk/jobs

3 TEACHING IN THE LIFELONG LEARNING SECTOR

Introduction

In this chapter you will learn about:
- roles and responsibilities
- teaching, learning and assessing
- challenges and barriers

Roles and responsibilities

Your main role as a teacher should be to teach your subject in a way that actively involves and engages your students during every session. You should use clear language at an appropriate level and in terms students will understand, motivating them to want to learn more. You should also manage the learning process from when your students commence to when they complete. How you do this will depend upon your subject, the age and experience of your students and the environment within which you will teach. Becoming a good teacher includes being enthusiastic and passionate about your subject, being approachable and taking pride in your work, all of which will be conveyed to your students through your teaching approaches.

A good first impression will help you to establish a positive working relationship with your students. The way you dress, act, respond to questions, offer support, etc. will also influence your students. They don't need to know anything personal about you, but they will probably make assumptions about you. If you are asked personal questions, try not to give out any information and don't be tempted to join students' social networking sites. By remaining a professional, and not becoming too friendly, you will retain their respect. Establishing routines will help your sessions flow smoothly, for example, always starting on time, setting and keeping to time limits for activities and breaks, and finishing on time.

The teaching and learning cycle

The teaching and learning cycle is so called as it can start at any stage and keep on going, however, all stages must be addressed for teaching and learning to be effective.

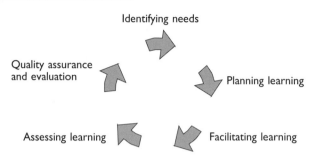

Figure 3.1 The teaching and learning cycle

Your role will usually follow the cycle and briefly involve:

- Identifying needs – finding out what your organisation's, your own, and potential students' needs are, interviewing students, carrying out initial assessments, ascertaining learning styles, agreeing individual learning plans with students.

- Planning learning – preparing a scheme of work, session plans and teaching and learning materials to ensure you cover the requirements of the syllabus, liaising with others, referring students to others for support if necessary.

- Facilitating learning – carrying out icebreakers, establishing ground rules, teaching and facilitating learning using a variety of approaches and methods, taking the register, keeping records of what was taught, acting professionally and with integrity, being qualified and/or experienced to teach your subject, using new technology where possible.

- Assessing learning – preparing assessment activities, checking your students have gained the necessary skills and knowledge at a given point, marking and giving feedback, maintaining relevant records.

- Quality assurance and evaluation – obtaining feedback from students, evaluating yourself and the programme in order to make improvements, attending meetings, maintaining your own professional development and subject currency. Evaluation should also be an ongoing process throughout all stages of the cycle.

Most teachers follow the cycle from beginning to end; however, your job role might not require you to be involved with all aspects. For example, you might only carry out the facilitating learning aspect of the cycle if you teach a programme which has been designed by someone else. You will probably undertake a variety of roles during your teaching career, each having various responsibilities or duties that you must carry out. The job roles do not relate to whether you are employed full-time or part-time, but to the duties you will perform.

To teach effectively involves not only the approaches you use to teach your subject, but many other factors that go before and after the taught session. This includes planning your sessions, preparing your teaching materials, assessing your students, marking work, giving feedback and evaluating yourself and your delivery.

Activity

Make a list of all the aspects you consider your role as a teacher will involve. What responsibilities will you have for each and why? If you have access to the internet, search for job descriptions in the Lifelong Learning Sector and compare these to your considerations.

Teaching, learning and assessing

You might feel you have the skills and knowledge to teach your subject to anyone, however, if learning doesn't take place you won't have done your job effectively. Teaching, learning and assessment approaches will differ depending upon the *subject* you are teaching, the *context* and *environment* you are teaching in and the *length* of each session. However, you should choose approaches which will engage, stimulate and motivate your students. It's not about what *you* will teach, but how *your* students will learn.

Example

Sanjay had planned to deliver a one-hour geography session to 16 students. He wanted to tell them about river and lake formation. Sanjay was really passionate about this topic and spoke continuously for 40 minutes. He then asked his students some questions which they were unable to answer. What he should have done was introduce the topic, then ask if any students knew about river and lake formation already. He could then have involved them and others with discussions. He should also have broken up his talk by showing pictures. He could have used some activities such as asking his students to draw diagrams or to look up aspects in books or on the internet. If he had broken his session into various stages, with different activities, learning would have been more successful.

Teaching

To be a good teacher involves not only having the skills and knowledge of your specialist subject, but the ability and enthusiasm to communicate this to others. While you might be extremely knowledgeable and experienced at your subject, until you try and teach it to someone else, you won't really know if you are good at it, or even if you enjoy it. If you decide to take the PTLLS

Award, you will be given the opportunity to teach for short periods in front of your peers, known as micro teaching sessions. This will give you a good idea of your capability and whether you enjoy teaching or not. If you do enjoy it, your passion and enthusiasm will be conveyed to your students, hopefully helping them enjoy the process as well as ensuring learning takes place.

When you are teaching others, you need to decide what it is they need to know, and then decide how you will deliver it. If you are teaching a qualification, there will be a syllabus or qualification handbook for you to follow. This will give you some guidance as to what you should teach. However, you might be able to decide what you will teach, along with the approaches you will use. If your subject is theoretical, you could use lectures, presentations and discussions. If your subject is practical, you could use demonstrations, activities and role plays. What you do need to consider is how your students will learn, based on the approaches you will use to teach. If you can use a variety of approaches when teaching, this will give your students more chances to be involved and ask questions. See Table 3.1 for some examples.

Table 3.1 Examples of teaching and learning approaches

Teaching	Learning
lecture	listening
presentation	watching and listening
discussion	listening, asking questions, voicing opinions
demonstration	watching, listening, asking questions
activities and practical application	realistic involvement, discussion, asking questions, problem solving
role plays	watching, listening, practical involvement
instruction	watching, listening, asking questions, attempting a task

Environments

A suitable environment is crucial for effective learning to take place. This involves not only the venue and resources used, but also your attitude and the support you give to your students. While learning can take place almost anywhere, not all environments will be totally suitable; however, it's *how* you teach your subject that will help make learning effective.

You may be restricted by the availability of some rooms or resources; therefore you need to be imaginative with what you do have. Your students don't need to know any problems your organisation has, as your professionalism should enable you to teach your subject effectively. However, you do need to take into account any health and safety issues and let your organisation know of any concerns. Perhaps you could change the layout of the room, for example, placing desks in groups rather than in rows. This would enable more effective communication to take place between students. However, you need to make sure you can see everyone, and they can see you.

You need to establish a purposeful learning environment where your students feel safe, secure, confident and valued. The venue, toilets and refreshment areas should be accessible and suitable to everyone. If your session includes a break, make sure you tell your students what time this will be and for how long. If you don't, your students may not be concentrating on their learning but thinking about when they can go to the toilet or get a drink.

Activity

Consider what teaching approaches you could use for your subject and why. If you plan to teach an accredited qualification, search the awarding organisation's website for a copy of the syllabus and have a look through it for ideas. What type of environment will you teach in and how will this impact upon the teaching and learning methods you use?

Scheme of work

To teach your subject effectively, you need to plan what you are going to do and when. A scheme of work (sometimes referred to as a *learning programme* or *scheme of learning*) is a document you can use to structure the teaching of your subject in a progressive way. The content should be flexible to allow for any changes, for example, a cancelled session due to adverse weather, and detailed enough in case a colleague needs to cover for you.

A scheme of work will usually contain headings such as:

Programme/qualification		Group composition		Dates from to
Number of sessions		Contact hours Non-contact hours		Venue
Aim of programme				
Dates	Objectives		Activities and resources	Assessment

You might like to put yourself in the place of the *student* when you are planning the order of what you will teach for each session. This way you can see things from a beginner's perspective to ensure you *keep things simple* during the earlier sessions. Otherwise, you might tend to want to achieve too much too soon, which could confuse your students. Even though it's very clear to you, you need to remember your students are hearing this for this first time. Always ask yourself, *What am I going to do with my students and why?*

There are certain aspects to consider when you are creating your scheme of work. For example, do you need to:

- obtain a syllabus to ascertain what will be taught?
- know the dates and times when students will be attending?
- obtain any information or resources?
- know details about your students, e.g. age range, ability, prior knowledge, learning styles?
- allow time for an induction, initial assessment, icebreaker and ground rules in the first session?
- devise delivery and assessment materials?
- allow time during the last session for an evaluation to take place?

Your scheme of work should show a variety of teaching and learning activities to suit all learning styles. Your sessions should follow in a logical order, which might not be the order printed in the syllabus.

Make sure you check all dates carefully in case there are any bank or public holidays on the days you would normally teach. The first session should include an induction to the programme and organisation, an icebreaker to help your students get to know each other, and the setting of ground rules, for example, timekeeping and switching off electronic devices. You might also need to assess prior learning and knowledge in this session, or before your students commence the programme. All subsequent sessions should begin with a recap of the previous session and allow time for questions, and end with an explanation of the next session. The final session should include an evaluation activity to obtain feedback from your students which will help you improve in future. You should also give details of how your students can progress further, i.e. what steps they can take to further their development. You may need to check if you will have the same venue for all the sessions, and what facilities, equipment and resources will be available. The more time you take to plan your scheme of work, the easier it will be to create your session plans.

Session plan

A session plan is a detailed breakdown of each date on your scheme of work. It will outline all the teaching and learning approaches you will use, with allocated timings, assessment activities and resources required. It will also take into account the individual requirements of your students. For example, if you have a student with dyslexia you will need to find out how you can support their learning.

A session plan will usually contain headings such as:

Teacher		Date		Venue	
Subject		Time and duration		Number of students	
Aim of session					
Group compos- ition					

Timing	Objectives	Resources	Teacher activities	Student activities	Assessment

A session plan should be produced prior to each teaching session and relate to the content on your scheme of work. Although it's very similar to the scheme of work, it is much more detailed and helps you manage the time that you are with your students. You need to consider what you want your students to be able to *know* or *do* by the end of the session; this is your *aim*. For example, *students will switch on a computer and access the internet*. Once you have a set of session plans, you can easily adapt them in the future for different groups of students, rather than starting again.

Each plan should have an introduction, development and summary; in other words, a beginning, middle and end, with times allocated to the activities within each. Your introduction should include the aim of the session and a recap of the previous session (if applicable). This should hopefully arouse interest and link to previous learning. You could carry out a *starter activity* to gain attention and focus learning. This could be a question to be discussed in pairs or groups, or a quiz based on what was learnt during the last session. If this is your first meeting with your students, make sure you introduce yourself, explain the facilities of the organisation, the requirements of the programme, carry out an icebreaker and agree the ground rules. You can also carry out any practical matters such as taking the register, or reminding students of any important issues.

The development stage is the teaching of your subject and this should be in a logical sequence for learning to progress. Imagine you are teaching someone to make a cup of tea. You can probably do it without thinking; however, to instruct a student who hasn't done it before you need to appreciate just how many steps are involved. It's the same with your subject; you know it well, but to teach a new student you need to break it down into smaller logical steps. These steps are usually based around the *learning outcomes* from the syllabus. If you don't have a syllabus, you can create your own learning outcomes or use objectives based upon your aim.

Example

Aim: students will:
- *switch on a computer and access the internet*

Objectives: students will:
- *locate a suitable computer and switch the power on*

- *use a keyboard and mouse to locate appropriate icons on the screen*

- *access the internet*

- *search for a particular website*

Objectives are always verbs, i.e. activities that can be demonstrated by your students. This ensures they will be doing something, and also ensures you can assess what they have done to check that learning has taken place.

You should include a variety of theory and practical approaches, activities and assessments to help maintain motivation and interest. You need to engage and include all your students by asking questions, holding discussions and carrying out activities. If you don't vary your activities they may become bored, lose concentration or be disruptive. Don't expect too much from your students at first, they don't have your knowledge and will need time to assimilate new knowledge and skills. Don't forget to allow time for a break if necessary. Before concluding your session, you might like to ask questions to check knowledge (one aimed at each student if you have time). If you have a large group, you could split them into teams and ask questions in the form of a quiz. This is a fun way of ending the session and shows you how much learning has taken place.

Your summary should include a recap of your original aim and relate it to what has been achieved. You should allow time for any questions from students and to discuss any homework or other issues. You can then state what the aim of your next session will be (if applicable).

Be prepared – better to have too much than not enough. Unused material can be carried forward to another session or given as homework. Also, consider students who may finish tasks early: can you give them something more challenging to do?

You should always evaluate your session; this could be afterwards when you have time to reflect, and/or by making notes as you progress. For example, if something didn't work well you could put a cross next to it on your session plan. You could note your strengths, areas for development and any action and improvements required for the future. Your plan may even change as you progress through your session to take into account the needs of your students. This is quite normal, so don't feel you have to keep to the original timings you allocated. If an activity is going well you can let it continue, or if it isn't, you can cut it short.

Aspects to consider when creating your session plan include:

- the overall aim – what you expect your students to achieve during this session
- group composition – details of individual students and needs to enable differentiation to take place
- objectives – how your students will achieve your aim – how do they link to the syllabus, in what order will you teach them, what timings will you allocate to each? Remember to include breaks if applicable
- resources – what you need to effectively teach your session – do you need to check or reserve anything in advance? Do you have a contingency plan?
- teacher activities – what you will be doing. Use a variety of theory and practical approaches to meet all learning styles
- student activities – what your students will be doing and for how long – how will you keep them motivated? How will you ensure the inclusion of all? Do you have spare activities in case some students finish before others? What could you remove if you run out of time?
- assessment – how will you assess that learning has taken place?
- the next session – how will you link the sessions?

Resources
Resources include all the aids, books, handouts, items of equipment, objects and people that you can use to deliver and assess your subject. They should

stimulate learning, add impact and promote interest in the subject. Resources should be accessible and inclusive to all students, while enabling them to acquire new skills and knowledge. When you are using or creating resources, ensure they promote equality of opportunity, reflect diversity and challenge stereotypes. Resources should be appropriate in terms of level, quality, quantity and content and be relevant to the subject and the learning expected. Handouts and presentations should be checked for spelling, grammar, punctuation and sentence construction errors. If you give a handout at the beginning of the session you may find your students fiddle with it and become distracted. If you can, issue them at an appropriate time and talk through the content, asking questions to ensure your students have understood. Otherwise, issue them at the end of the session and ask students to read them later to help reinforce what has been covered during the session. Handouts can also be used as activities, for example, a *gapped handout* can contain sentences with missing words that students need to fill in. These are useful to test lower level students, as a fun team activity or to fill in time at the end of a session. If a resource you are using is not effective with some students, try changing the experience rather than the resource. You might need to explain the resource differently or change a group activity to become an individual one or vice versa. You should also consider how you can embed new technology into your sessions. This can be either for use by yourself, for example, an interactive whiteboard, and/or for use by your students, for example, using laptops or mobile devices for internet research. You would need to feel confident yourself using ICT equipment and may therefore need further training. You would also need to ensure everything is accessible, in working order and appropriate for your students.

Examples of resources include:

- audio/digital/visual equipment
- books, catalogues, journals, magazines
- computerised presentations
- computers
- flip chart paper and pens
- handouts
- interactive or electronic whiteboards
- people: specialist speakers; colleagues
- physical resources, models and apparatus
- projectors
- radios/televisions/mobile phones

- textbooks

- worksheets, puzzles and crosswords

Preparing for unforeseen circumstances comes with experience. Whenever you are due to teach a session, ask yourself: *What would I do if something wasn't available or doesn't work?* You might prepare a computerised presentation and make copies as handouts that you can give your students. However, if you can't get copies made in time, you can still deliver your presentation and offer to e-mail a copy to your students.

Activity

What resources could you use to teach your subject and why? Research new and emerging technologies to see what is available to support your specialist subject.

Communication

Communication is a means of passing on information from one person to another. It is also a manner of expression, for example, your body language, your voice and the gestures you make. The first time you meet your students they will probably make a subconscious judgement about you, and you will probably make one of them. These judgements often turn out to be wrong; therefore it is important not to make any assumptions.

Body language includes facial expressions, eye contact, gestures, posture, non-verbal signals and appearance. Your personality will show through when you are teaching. However, there are some aspects you might not be able to control, such as facial flushing, blinking or clearing your throat. Nevertheless, some you should be able to control, such as winking, giving a thumbs-up sign or laughing. You need to be aware of not only your own body language, but also that of your students. You need to sense what they are not saying as well as what they are saying.

Communication is the key to encouraging student motivation, managing behaviour and disruption, and becoming a successful teacher. It should always be appropriate and effective, and pitched to the level of your students. If you need to write on a board or flip chart while speaking to your students, don't do both at the same time. If you face the board, they may not hear you speak and you might miss something happening in the room.

Successful communication includes:

- oral communication, i.e. the way you speak when you are explaining, describing, summarising, questioning and giving feedback – be aware of your voice projection, tone and accent and when to use pauses to gain attention or allow thinking time

- written communication, i.e. presentations, handouts, worksheets, written feedback and progress reports – always check your spelling, grammar, punctuation and sentence construction

- non-verbal communication, i.e. the way you act, your body language, appearance, facial expressions, eye contact, gestures, posture and non-verbal signals

- questioning, i.e. oral or written, to include all students, preferably using open questions beginning with who, what, when, where, why and how

- listening skills, i.e. eye contact, not interrupting, not being judgemental

- skills such as empathy and sympathy

The language you use should reflect equality and inclusiveness, be relevant to the subject, not offend anyone in any way and be at the right level and pitch for your students. You may have to practise with your voice projection, but don't shout, just speak a little louder and slower than normal and ask if students can hear you. Don't expect your students to remember everything first time; they don't know what *you* know. You should repeat or rephrase key points regularly. You might even get frustrated if you are asked questions regarding points you have already explained. Try not to say things like, *I just told you that or Can't you remember what I just said?* Repeating key points will help your students remember them, as will asking them questions to check their knowledge. Don't embarrass a student in front of their peer group; they may feel they can't ask you anything again. Learning occurs best in an active, not a passive environment where communication is a two-way process.

Try and minimise any barriers to communication, for example, background noise, seating positions or the way you explain a topic. If a student asks a question, repeat this when you answer it so that everyone can hear what was asked, along with your answer. The same applies if a student answers a question, as not everyone may hear the answer. Encourage your students to ask you questions, no matter how silly they think they are; probably the person sitting next to them is thinking the same but daren't ask. If you are asked something you don't know the answer to, say you will find out later and then make sure you do. Don't feel you have to know everything and don't bluff your way through something as you will inevitably be found out.

Learning

Students may have a particular *learning style,* a way that helps them to learn which is based on listening, seeing and doing. Your students could take a short learning styles test prior to commencing, to identify their preferred styles. There are many free tests available via the internet. However, what you may tend to do is teach your sessions in the style in which you learn best – although it will suit you, it may not suit your students.

Fleming (2005) stated that people can be grouped according to four styles of learning: visual, aural, read/write and kinaesthetic (VARK).

Visual examples (seeing) – students usually:

- are meticulous and neat in appearance
- find verbal instructions difficult
- memorise by looking at pictures
- notice details
- observe rather than act or talk
- like watching videos/DVDs

Aural examples (listening and talking) – students usually:

- are easily distracted
- enjoy talking and listening to others
- have difficulty with written instructions
- hum, sing and whisper or talk out loud
- ask questions
- don't like noisy environments

Read/write examples (reading and writing) – students usually:

- are good spellers and have good handwriting
- enjoy research
- like rewriting what others have written
- like to read books
- use a dictionary and thesaurus
- write lists and make notes

Kinaesthetic examples (doing) – students usually:

- are tactile towards others
- do not like reading and are often poor spellers

- enjoy worksheets and discussions
- fidget with pens while studying
- like practical activities
- use their hands while talking

Most students are multimodal, i.e. a mixture of two or more styles enabling learning to take place more quickly.

When you start teaching, you may find you are teaching in the same way you were taught at school or college. This could be lecturing, reading from a book or writing information on a board, which might not have been very effective for your own learning. You won't yet know all the other approaches you could use to make learning interesting and engaging. Active learning helps people remember, passive learning may lead them to forget. As you become more experienced at teaching, your confidence will grow and you will be able to experiment with different approaches, as not all teaching methods suit all students.

There is an old Chinese proverb: *I hear – I forget; I see – I remember; I do – I understand.* When you hear lots of information you may find it difficult to remember it all. If you can see something taking place that represents what you hear, you will hopefully remember more. However, if you actually carry out the task, you will understand the full process and remember how to do it again.

Studies show that over a period of three days, learning retention is as follows:

- *10% of what you read*
- *20% of what you hear*
- *30% of what you see*
- *50% of what you see and hear*
- *70% of what you say*
- *90% of what you say and do*

(Pike, 1989)

Therefore, if you can enable your students to carry out practical activities to put theory into practice, they will begin to understand what they have learnt.

The following table gives some examples of how you could use different teaching approaches to reach all learning styles.

Table 3.2: Examples of learning styles

Topic	Visual	Aural	Read/write	Kinaesthetic
Answering the telephone	Watching a demonstration, viewing a presentation and video	Listening to instructions, asking questions	Making notes, reading instructions and handouts	Carrying out the task or a role play
Decorating a cake	Watching a demonstration, viewing a presentation and video	Listening to instructions, asking questions	Making notes, reading instructions and handouts	Carrying out the task
Remembering historical dates	Viewing a video	Listening to instructions, discussing with others	Reading text-books and handouts, writing facts and dates	Researching the internet, carrying out a role play
Practising interview skills	Viewing a video or simulation	Listening to instructions, asking questions	Reading hand-outs, making notes	Carrying out a role play
Using a word processor	Watching a demonstration, viewing a presentation and video	Listening to instructions, asking questions	Making notes, reading instructions and handouts	Carrying out the task
Learning a foreign language	Viewing a video	Listening to conversations and record-ings of people speaking, talking to others	Reading text-books, writing words and phrases	Holding a con-versation
Changing a fuse	Watching a demonstration, viewing a presentation and video	Listening to instructions, asking questions	Making notes, reading instructions	Carrying out the task

Activity

Think about the subject you will teach. What activities could your students do to cover the visual, aural, read/write and kinaesthetic learning styles? If you have access to the internet, carry out the free five-minute learning styles test at www.vark-learn.com and see which style you are. This is a test you could ask your future students to carry out as the results will help you plan which teaching and learning methods to use.

Attention spans

An attention span is the amount of time that a student can concentrate without being distracted. This will vary according to the ages of your students; younger students may concentrate less and older ones more. Being able to focus without being distracted is crucial for learning to take place. There are two types of attention, *focused* and *sustained*.

- Focused attention is a short-term response to something that attracts awareness and is very brief, for example, the ring of a telephone or an unexpected occurrence. After a few seconds, it is likely that the person will return to what they were originally doing or think about something else.

- Sustained attention is a longer-term response which will enable the achievement of something over a period of time. For example, if the task is to take a few photos, choose the best three and upload them to a website, then the person showing sustained attention will stay on task and achieve it. A person who loses attention might take a few photos but move on to doing something else before choosing and uploading the best three.

Most healthy teenagers and adults are able to sustain attention on one thing for about 20 minutes (Cornish and Dukette, 2009: 73). They can then choose to refocus on the same thing for another 20 minutes. This ability to renew concentration enables people to stay on task for as long as necessary. However, there are other factors to take into consideration, such as self-motivation, ability, family issues, tiredness and hunger. If a student is hungry or thirsty their concentration may lapse as a result. If you find your students losing focus, ask them if there's anything distracting them as you might be able to resolve it, for example, by opening a window if it's too warm.

When planning to deliver your sessions, try and use lots of short tasks to enable your students to stay focused. If you do need to use longer tasks, try and break these down into 20 minutes for each, with chance for a discussion or something different in between. If you teach long sessions, for example, over an hour, try and include a break to enable your students to experience a change of scenery, obtain refreshments and visit the toilet if necessary.

Example

Barbara was working on her session plan for her group of Hair and Beauty students. She was due to teach the unit Promote Products and Services to Clients in a Salon for one hour. She decided she would introduce the unit for five minutes, involve her students in a discussion for ten minutes, then facilitate a research activity for 20 minutes. This would be followed by a further discussion for five minutes and a role play activity for 15 minutes. She had a final five minutes for a summary and questions. During the session Barbara was able to keep her students busy with a variety of activities. She could also check that learning was taking place by observing their actions and asking questions.

Assessing

Assessment is a way of finding out if learning has taken place. It enables you to ascertain if your student has gained the required skills, competence, knowledge, understanding and/or attitudes needed at a given point. It is therefore a process of making a decision regarding your student's knowledge and/or performance against set criteria. Whatever you are assessing, you need to have the confidence to make a decision and convey this to your students. Assessment should focus on improving and reinforcing learning as well as measuring achievements. It should help your students realise how they are progressing and what they need to do to improve and/or progress further.

The assessment process is a systematic procedure which should be followed to give your students a positive experience. Depending upon the subject you are assessing and whether it is academic (theory or knowledge based) or vocational (practical or performance based), you will usually follow the assessment cycle (see Figure 3.2). The cycle will continue until all aspects of the qualification or programme have been successfully achieved by your student, or they leave. Records must be maintained throughout to satisfy your organisation, the regulatory authorities and awarding organisations.

Figure 3.2 The assessment cycle

- Initial assessment – ascertaining if your student has any previous knowledge or experience of the subject or topic to be assessed. This information can be obtained through application forms, discussions and interviews. The results of initial assessment activities will give you information regarding your students; for example, any specific assessment requirements they may have, their learning style or any further training and support they may need. This process might not always be carried out by you, but the information obtained must be passed on to you.

- Assessment planning – agreeing suitable methods of assessment with each student, setting appropriate target dates, involving others as necessary, for example, colleagues or supervisors, and following relevant organisational guidelines.

- Assessment activity – these relate to the methods used, i.e. assessor led, for example, observation or questioning; or student led, for example, completing assignments, writing statements or gathering appropriate evidence of competence. Assessment can be formative (ongoing) and/or summative (at the end).

- Assessment decision and feedback – making a judgement of success or otherwise. Giving constructive feedback and agreeing any further action that may be necessary. Records of what was assessed and the decisions made should always be maintained.

- Review of progress – the assessment plan can be reviewed and updated at any time until your student completes or decides to leave. Reviewing progress with your students will give you an opportunity to discuss any other issues that may be relevant to their progress. Reviewing the assessment activities used will give you the opportunity to amend them if necessary.

The cycle will then begin again with an initial assessment regarding the next topic or unit of the qualification. Throughout the cycle, standardisation of assessment practice between assessors should take place; this will help ensure the consistency and fairness of decisions and that everyone interprets the requirements in the same way. If the qualification is accredited by an awarding organisation, internal and external quality assurance must take place to ensure the assessment process is fair and effective.

Assessment should not be confused with evaluation; assessment is of the *student*, evaluation is of the *programme* that the student is taking, for example, the learning experience. Assessment is specific towards students' achievements and how they can improve. Evaluation is a quality assurance monitoring tool. It includes obtaining feedback from your students and others, for example, employers, line managers and quality assurers to help improve the overall student experience as well as your own practice.

There is a difference between assessment *for* learning, and assessment *of* learning. Assessment *for* learning is usually a formative process. It will ascertain progress so far in order to plan further learning and development. Assessment *of* learning is usually summative and confirms that learning has taken place.

Example

Phenal devised a multiple-choice quiz for his students to carry out at the end of one of his maths sessions. He had devised several questions for his students to answer individually on paper. This formative assessment helped him gauge how his students had progressed at a given point in time. It was a non-threatening way of assessing his students' progress. It helped him to plan what further learning his students needed before taking the final summative test.

Table 3.3 gives examples of formative and summative assessment methods which could be used. Formative methods are usually devised by the teacher, whereas summative methods are usually devised by the awarding organisation.

Table 3.3 Examples of formative and summative assessment activities

Topic	Formative	Summative
Answering the telephone	Role play	Observation and questions
Decorating a cake	Practical activity	Observation and questions
Remembering historical dates	Multiple-choice quiz	Essay or exam
Practising interview skills	Role play	Observation and questions
Using a word processor	Practical activity on own	Test
Learning a foreign language	Practical activity in pairs	Discussion
Changing a fuse	Practical activity	Observation and questions

Activity

Consider the subject you will assess. What formative and summative activities could you use and why?

Giving feedback

All students need to know how they are progressing and what they have achieved at regular points. Giving feedback will help encourage, motivate and develop them further. This can be given after an assessment activity, perhaps verbally to your student; however, it should always be formally documented afterwards. When giving feedback in writing, it should be written on the correct document, not just written on your student's work, in case they lose it. Feedback should be based on facts which relate to what has been assessed and should not be based purely on your personal opinions. The former is known as *objective*, the latter *subjective*. However, you can mix the two. For example, *Well done, Tricia, you have met the criteria and I felt the way you handled the situation was really professional.*

The advantages of giving feedback are:

- it creates opportunities for clarification, discussion and progression
- it emphasises progress rather than failure
- it can boost your student's confidence and motivation
- it identifies further learning opportunities or actions required
- your student knows what they have achieved
- your student knows what they need to improve or change

Verbal feedback should be a two-way process, allowing a discussion to take place to clarify any points and plan further actions if necessary. Consider your tone of voice and take into account your student's non-verbal signals and your own body language. You might give feedback to a group regarding an activity; if so, make sure your feedback is specific to the group, and/or each individual's contributions. Your students will like to know how they are progressing, and what they need to do to improve or develop further. Simple statements such as 'well done' or 'good' don't tell your student *what* was well done or good about their work or *how* they can improve it. Using your student's name makes the feedback more personal, being specific enables your student to see what they need to do to improve, and smiling while giving feedback can be encouraging.

Feedback should always be:

- based on facts and not opinions
- clear, genuine and unambiguous
- constructive and developmental – giving examples for improvement or further development

- documented – records must be maintained

- focused on the activity not the person

- given as soon as possible

- helpful and supportive

- honest, specific and detailed regarding what was or wasn't achieved

Often, the focus of feedback is likely to be on mistakes rather than strengths. If something positive is stated first, any negative comments are more likely to be listened to and acted upon. Starting with a negative point may discourage your student from listening to anything else that is said. If possible, start with something positive, then state what could be improved, and finish on a developmental note. This sandwiches the negative aspect between two positive or helpful aspects, and is known as the *praise sandwich*. You will need to find out if your organisation has any specific feedback methods they wish you to use which will ensure a standardised approach across all assessors to all students. If assessment decisions count towards the achievement of a qualification, it is crucial to keep your feedback records, along with any action identified for each student. Records must always be kept safe as organisations expect them to be securely managed, whether they are manual or electronic.

Challenges and barriers

You will face many challenges and barriers when teaching, for example:

- disruptive students

- lack of information

- lack of time for preparation and marking

- limited resources and budgets

- unsupportive colleagues

Your students may also experience issues which could impact upon their learning, for example, their:

- faith, culture and religion

- family and home circumstances and commitments

- fears, for example, technology, change, not knowing anyone else in the group

- limited basic skills

- previous negative experiences of learning

- transport arrangements

Hopefully you can identify these early on to be able to address them. However, other issues may occur during the programme and you would need to plan a suitable course of action to help yourself or your students' progress in an appropriate way. With any issues, you need to remain in control, be fair and ethical with all your students and not demonstrate any favouritism towards particular ones, for example, by giving one more support than others. You might feel it sensible to make a telephone call to a student who has been absent but making regular calls would be inappropriate. Giving your personal telephone number to students could be seen as encouraging informal contact, and you may get calls or texts which are not suitable or relevant. You might not want to take your break with your students or join their social networking sites as you could become more of a friend than a teacher. It is unprofessional to use bad language, to touch students in an inappropriate way or to let your personal problems affect your work. You might have professional boundaries which could affect your role, for example, the amount of paperwork you are expected to complete or the lack of funding or resources. Boundaries can often be interpreted as the negative aspects to your role and responsibilities.

Motivation and behaviour

Motivation is either *intrinsic* (from within), meaning the student wants to learn for their own fulfilment, or *extrinsic* (from without), meaning there may be an external factor motivating them, for example, a promotion at work.

Many factors affect a student's motivation to work and to learn, for example, interest in the subject matter, perception of its usefulness, a general desire to achieve, self-confidence and self-esteem, as well as patience and persistence. Not all students are motivated by the same values, needs, desires, or wants. Some of your students will be motivated by the approval of others, some by overcoming personal challenges.

Whatever level of motivation your students have will be transformed, for better or worse, by what happens during their experience with you. You therefore need to promote a professional relationship that leads to individual learning based on honesty and trust. Some students may seem naturally enthusiastic about learning, but many need or expect you to inspire, motivate, challenge, engage and stimulate them.

To get through a session without any disruptions would be wonderful, but this very rarely happens. You might have a student who arrives late, an inquisitive student who always wants to know more, or just someone asking to leave the room to get a drink of water. Whatever the disruption may be, you need to handle this professionally to minimise any effect it may have on teaching and learning. Don't just ignore the behaviour, address it immediately. However, with experience you will realise that some things can be ignored providing this does not affect the safety of your students.

Example

Cameron was giving a presentation to a group of 20 students during a Monday morning session. Two students in the group started talking among themselves. Rather than reprimand them in front of their peers, Cameron decided to stop speaking altogether and use eye contact with them. They soon realised he was no longer speaking to everyone but looking at them. Because he was silent, they stopped talking and paid attention again.

Usually, disruptions or changes in behaviour occur because a student doesn't follow the ground rules; for example, their mobile phone rings, or they do something other than that which you have asked them to do. If this is the case, politely ask them to stop, remind them of the ground rules and how they are also disrupting their peers' learning. Other occurrences happen because people are bored, they don't understand what you are saying, their attention span is low, or you are not challenging them enough. You could give an alternative activity to stretch and challenge learning, get them involved with other students in an activity, or have a quick one-to-one chat to find out why they are behaving that way.

Activity

What challenges and barriers do you think you will encounter when you start teaching? How can you remain professional while dealing with these?

Summary

In this chapter you have learnt about:

- roles and responsibilities
- teaching, learning and assessing
- challenges and barriers

Theory focus
References and further information

Appleyard, N and Appleyard, K (2010) *Communicating with Students in the Lifelong Learning Sector.* Exeter: Learning Matters.

Clark, T (2010) *Mental Health Matters for FE: Teachers' Toolkit.* Leicester: NIACE.

Cornish, D and Dukette D, (2009) *The Essential 20: Twenty Components of an Excellent Health Care Team.* Pittsburgh: RoseDog Books.

Fleming, N (2005) *Teaching and learning styles: VARK strategies.* Honolulu: Honolulu Community College.

Gravells, A (2012) *Achieving your TAQA Assessor and Internal Quality Assurer Award.* London: Learning Matters.

Gravells, A (2012) *Preparing to Teach in the Lifelong Learning Sector: The New Award* (5th edition). London: Learning Matters.

Gravells, A and Simpson, S (2012) *Equality and Diversity in the Lifelong Learning Sector.* London: Learning Matters.

Hill, C, (2008) *Teaching with e-learning in the Lifelong Learning Sector* (2nd edition). Exeter: Learning Matters.

Pike, R W (1989) *Creative Training Techniques Handbook.* Minneapolis MN: Lakewood Books.

Powell, S and Tummons, J (2011) *Inclusive Practice in the Lifelong Learning Sector.* Exeter: Learning Matters.

Vizard, D (2007) *How to Manage Behaviour in Further Education.* London: Sage Publications Ltd.

Wallace, S (2007) *Managing Behaviour in the Lifelong Learning Sector* (2nd edition). Exeter: Learning Matters.

Websites

Attention spans – http://news.bbc.co.uk/1/hi/1834682.stm

Carr N (2010) The Web Shatters Focus, Rewires Brains, *Wired magazine*, 24 May 2010 – www.wired.com/magazine/2010/05/ff.nicholas.carr/all/1

Learning styles test – www.vark-learn.com

Support for adult students – www.direct.gov.uk/adultlearning

Introduction

In this chapter you will learn about:
- The Institute for Learning
- The minimum core
- Associate and Qualified Teacher status

The Institute for Learning (IfL)

The Institute for Learning (IfL) is the professional body for teachers, tutors, trainers and student teachers in the Lifelong Learning Sector. It was created in 2002 by teachers in further education, trade unions and employer bodies such as the Association of Colleges. The IfL see teachers and trainers not as a workforce, but as professionals.

The IfL is operated by members for members, and celebrates the diverse nature of the sector, including: Adult and Community Learning, Emergency and Public Services, Further Education Colleges, Ministry of Defence/Armed Services, the Voluntary Sector and Work-based Learning.

The IfL works to influence the national further education and skills agenda by building relationships with key decision makers, agencies and government departments. You can become a member of the IfL and have the opportunity to contribute to consultations regarding key policies, even if you haven't started teaching yet. You will then be able to access resources and information to help your teaching role.

All teachers and trainers working in publicly funded further education and skills provision in England are required to register as members with the IfL and undertake continuing professional development (CPD) every year. Registration should be within six months of starting a teaching role and the PTLLS Award should be achieved within one year. PTLLS Award holders will be classed as an *Affiliate* member until fully qualified as a teacher. Membership of the IfL does not give you your professional teaching status, a separate application process must be gone through called *professional formation* to achieve your Licence to Practise.

IfL Member grades

There are different grades of membership with the IfL depending upon your qualifications and experience. Associate, Member and Fellow grades enable you to use designatory letters after your name. The grades are:

- Companion
- Affiliate
- Associate (AIfL)
- Member (MIfL)
- Fellow (FIfL)

Companion

This grade is for anyone in a leadership, management or support role in the sector who is not a qualified teacher nor taking a teacher training qualification. It is also for those from non-teaching backgrounds who wish to be associated with the sector.

Affiliate

This category of membership is for those who are:

- interested in becoming a teacher in the Lifelong Learning Sector
- new to the teaching profession
- working towards the PTLLS Award
- in a learning support role

Associate (AIfL)

This category of membership is for those who are:

- experienced practitioners within further education and skills, who hold a minimum of:
  - the level 3 or 4 CTLLS qualification or equivalent, or
  - assessor awards

Associates can be eligible to work towards Associate Teacher Learning and Skills status (ATLS).

Member (MIfL)

This category of membership is for those who are:

- experienced practitioners within further education and skills, who hold a minimum of the level 5 Diploma (DTLLS) or equivalent.

Members are eligible to work towards Qualified Teacher Learning and Skills status (QTLS) or Associate Teacher Learning and Skills status (ATLS), according to their qualifications and teaching role.

Fellow (FIfL)

This category of membership is for those who are highly experienced practitioners within post-16 education and training, who hold higher degrees (Masters and Doctorates) in their specialist subject areas, in addition to their teaching qualification. Fellows are eligible to apply for QTLS or ATLS status according to their qualifications and teaching role.

Example

Two years ago Liang commenced the PTLLS Award and registered with the IfL as an Affiliate member. He then obtained an Associate Teacher position teaching First Aid on a part-time basis. He went on to take his CTLLS qualification and applied to the IfL to upgrade to a Member. He is now teaching full-time and plans to apply for his ATLS teaching status. This will confer his Licence to Practise once he has finished his probation period and completed the professional formation process.

Under the Teaching Regulations, the IfL provides the mechanism by which teachers register and progress through to being Licensed Practitioners. After the relevant teaching qualification has been obtained, teachers will undertake a period of probation before applying for their Licence to Practise. It is compulsory for all members to follow the IfL *Code of Professional Practice* (2008). The Code defines the professional behaviour which, in the public interest, the IfL expects of its members throughout their membership and professional career.

Code of Professional Practice

The Institute for Learning's Code of Professional Practice came into force on 1 April 2008. The Code was developed by the profession for the profession and it outlines the behaviours expected of members – for the benefit of students, employers, the profession and the wider community. The Code contains seven behaviours:

1. Professional integrity
2. Respect
3. Reasonable care
4. Professional practice
5. Criminal offence disclosure
6. Responsibility during Institute investigations
7. Responsibility to the Institute

Behaviour 1: Professional integrity

The members shall:

1. meet their professional responsibilities consistent with the Institute's Professional Values.

2. use reasonable professional judgement when discharging differing responsibilities and obligations to students, colleagues, institution and the wider profession.

3. uphold the reputation of the profession by never unjustly or knowingly damaging the professional reputation of another or furthering their own position unfairly at the expense of another.

4. comply with all reasonable assessment and quality procedures and obligations.

5. uphold the standing and reputation of the Institute and not knowingly undermine or misrepresent its views nor their Institute membership, any qualification or professional status.

Behaviour 2: Respect

The members shall at all times:

1. respect the rights of students and colleagues in accordance with relevant legislation and organisation requirements.

2. act in a manner which recognises diversity as an asset and does not discriminate in respect of race, gender, disability and/or learning difficulty, age, sexual orientation or religion and belief.

Behaviour 3: Reasonable care

The members shall take reasonable care to ensure the safety and welfare of students and comply with relevant statutory provisions to support their wellbeing and development.

Behaviour 4: Professional practice

The members shall provide evidence to the Institute that they have complied with the current Institute CPD policy and guidelines.

Behaviour 5: Criminal offence disclosure

Any member shall notify the Institute as soon as practicable after cautioning or conviction for a criminal offence. The Institute reserves the right to act on such information through its disciplinary process.

Behaviour 6: Responsibility during Institute investigations

A member shall use their best endeavours to assist in any investigation and shall not seek to dissuade, penalise or discourage a person from bringing a complaint against any member, interfere with or otherwise compromise due process.

Behaviour 7: Responsibility to the Institute

The members shall at all times act in accordance with the Institute's conditions of membership which will be subject to change from time to time.

(IfL Code of Professional Practice: raising concerns about IfL members, 2009:4)

There are four sanctions which can be applied to members who breach the Code of Professional Practice:

- a reprimand
- a conditional registration order
- a suspension order
- an expulsion order

Anyone can put in a complaint to the IfL if they have a legitimate reason. The nature of the sanction imposed will depend upon the circumstances of the case. If you think you have accidentally broken the Code, it's best to discuss this with the IfL before a complaint is made against you.

Licence to Practise

The Institute for Learning will issue a *Licence to Practise* as a teacher once certain requirements have been fulfilled. (It's 'practise' with an 's' as it's the verb 'to practise', in this context meaning 'to teach', i.e. a *Licence to Teach*, rather than 'practice' with a 'c', which is the noun – as with 'license/licence' and 'advise/advice', etc.)

First, you must obtain the relevant teaching qualifications and obtain evidence of achievement of the Minimum Core. The Minimum Core is the term given to literacy, language, numeracy and Information Communication Technology (ICT) skills. These are important skills that teachers must have, not only for themselves, but to support their students.

You must be teaching in a recognised Lifelong Learning organisation to enable you to complete the *professional formation* process. You can then apply to the IfL for your teaching status (ATLS/QTLS), which confers your Licence to Practise as an Associate or Full teacher. Once achieved, you maintain your Licence by partaking in and reflecting on relevant CPD activities.

It's only right that teachers should have a Licence to Practise as this conveys a professional image to their students. Many professions hold licences, for example, doctors, lawyers and accountants.

Licences to practise can take a number of forms, some voluntary and some mandatory. They include a measure of professional competence and behavioural standards such as a Code of Practice. They are concerned with permission to practise in an area of technical, craft or professional competence.

John Hayes, Minister of State for Further Education, Skills and Lifelong Learning, stated:

> *Professional standards, including occupational licensing, can be a powerful way of raising ambition in skills and training provision contributing to greater productivity and growth in a sector.*
>
> *[The next day at the parliamentary seminar on licence to practise, he said:] This is critically about driving the status of skills . . . gaining a licence to practise in a certain field can have a big effect on people's purpose and pride – an important component of any society.*
>
> (IfL *Intuition*, Issue 5, Summer 2011: 8)

Knowing that you have a Licence to Practise will give your students the confidence that they will get a professional and up-to-date service from their teacher. It should also give you pride in your job role.

The IfL will confer your Licence to Practise once you have fulfilled the following:

1. Gained a relevant teaching qualification (CTLLS *or* DTLLS/Cert Ed/PGCE)
2. Evidenced the Minimum Core
3. Maintained membership of the IfL
4. Carried out a probation period of teaching
5. Maintained continuing professional development (CPD)
6. Completed the IfL professional formation process

Your Licence to Practise as a teacher is gained by achieving Associate or Qualified Teacher status in the Lifelong Learning Sector (ATLS/QTLS).

Activity

If you haven't already done so, register with the Institute for Learning (IfL) online at www.ifl.ac.uk. This would be a good time to update your curriculum vitae to ensure you have all your dates and details handy. Have a look at the different pages on the IfL website to find out what support they give to teachers.

The minimum core

All teachers should have a knowledge and understanding of literacy, language, numeracy, and ICT skills to at least Level 2. These skills are known as the Minimum Core and will enable you to effectively fulfil your role as a professional teacher. The Minimum Core was introduced as part of The Further Education Teachers' Qualifications (England) Regulations (2007) to raise skills.

When you are teaching, your students will trust and believe you. If you spell words wrongly in a handout or presentation, your students will think the spelling is correct, just because you are their teacher. It's therefore important to give a good impression of yourself through your writing, numerical and computer skills. If you aim to achieve your Licence to Practise, you may need to pass external tests in these subjects beforehand. However, if you already hold a qualification which is equivalent to the Minimum Core, for example, Key Skills Level 2, you could be exempt. You can check if your qualification meets the requirements at the shortcut: http://tinyurl.com/cka789u

You might like to take additional learning programmes, for example, if your computer skills need further development or you feel your spelling, grammar or numeracy need improving. There are free online programmes you could access; see page 75 the end of the chapter for details.

Conversely, it's not just about your own skills in these areas; it's about being able to develop them in your students too. The trick is to do it without them realising.

Example

Aadi teaches plumbing and has realised that many aspects of the job include literacy, language, numeracy and ICT. Reading instructions and writing orders involve literacy, and talking to customers and suppliers includes language. Measuring pipes, calculating the amount of materials to use and working out invoices all include numeracy. Researching materials on the internet and e-mailing suppliers include the use of ICT. Aadi therefore embeds all these skills naturally with his students while teaching his subject.

Whenever you have the opportunity, help your students realise their mistakes; for example, when you are marking their work make sure you point out any misspelt words or inaccurate calculations. You can also encourage your students to use ICT, for example, researching topics via the internet.

If possible use activities which can embed aspects of the following skills within your teaching:

- Literacy and language – reading, writing, listening, presenting, speaking, discussing.
- Numeracy – approximations, estimations, calculations, measurements.

- ICT– e-mail, web-based research, word processing assignments and reports, using spreadsheets, databases and presentation packages.

Activity

What opportunities could you create to embed literacy, language, numeracy and ICT skills for your subject with your own students?

Access the Move-on website at www.move-on.org.uk/practicetests.asp, where you will find a selection of free literacy and numeracy National Test practice papers and resources. Successful completion of the National Tests at Level 2 could be used as evidence of your literacy and numeracy skills for the Minimum Core.

You can also undertake free computer training at http://learn.go-on.co.uk/

Associate and Qualified Teacher status

In 2007, Lifelong Learning UK (now the Learning and Skills Improvement Service) identified two distinct and important teacher roles in the Further Education sector in England:

- an *associate teaching* role, which has fewer teaching responsibilities and which will be performed by those who are expected to gain the status of Associate Teacher, Learning and Skills (ATLS)
- a *full teaching* role, which represents the full range of responsibilities performed by those who are expected to gain the status of Qualified Teacher, Learning and Skills (QTLS)

These roles were identified through extensive research into teacher roles in the sector. From September 2007 in England, it was no longer the amount of *time* that someone taught that determined which teaching qualification should be undertaken, but their *role* as a teacher. All those who teach, even on a part-time basis, are required to undertake a teaching qualification appropriate to either an *Associate* teacher role or a *Full* teacher role.

However, there is also an *Occasional Teacher* role, which is someone who teaches no more than 28 hours in a year. Occasional teachers are not subject to the existing regulations and therefore not required to be members of IfL, though they can join on a voluntary basis.

Example

Susan is a retired floristry teacher who occasionally covers classes at the college at which she used to teach. This only occurs if a member of staff is absent and her hours never total more than 20 a year. She is therefore classed as an occasional teacher.

Paul teaches health and safety on a part-time basis in community halls. The programme he delivers is a national one, meaning the students go through the same process no matter where they attend. Paul teaches using materials and resources prepared by someone else. He is therefore an associate teacher.

Ibrahim teaches engineering part-time in a training organisation. He prepares his own schemes of work, session plans and resources. Even though he is part-time, he still carries out the full teaching role, therefore he is classed as a full teacher.

The associate and full teaching roles have been described in the Further Education Teachers' Qualifications (England) Regulations (2007) as:

> *Associate teaching role means a teaching role that carries significantly less than the full range of teaching responsibilities ordinarily carried out in a full teaching role (whether on a full-time, part-time, fractional, fixed term, temporary or agency basis) and does not require the teacher to demonstrate an extensive range of knowledge, understanding and application of curriculum development, curriculum innovation or curriculum delivery strategies.*

> *Full teaching role means a teaching role that carries the full range of teaching responsibilities (whether on a full-time, part-time, fractional, fixed term, temporary or agency basis) and requires the teacher to demonstrate an extensive range of knowledge, understanding and application of curriculum development, curriculum innovation or curriculum delivery strategies.*
>
> (http://www.legislation.gov.uk/uksi/2007/2264/contents/made, accessed 9 December 2011)

To gain *Associate* or *Full* teacher status, you need to first register with the Institute for Learning (IfL), achieve the relevant teaching qualification for your job role (within five years), and fulfil the minimum core and continuing professional development (CPD) requirements. This is all part of your *professional formation*. If you teach in a nation other than England, you will need to ascertain what their particular requirements are.

Professional formation

To gain your Licence to Practise after achieving your teaching qualification you need to complete a period of probation known as *professional formation*. This is when you show, over a period of time, that you can apply your skills and knowledge effectively to meet the teaching standards.

Professional formation is:

> *...the post-qualification process by which a teacher demonstrates through professional practice:*
>
> 1. *the ability to use effectively the skills and knowledge acquired whilst training to be a teacher;*
> 2. *and the capacity to meet the occupational standards required of a teacher.*
>   (The Further Education Teachers' Qualifications (England) Regulations, 2007: 2)

You should have a mentor in the same subject specialism as your own who will give ongoing support and advice. They will then be able to endorse your request for your teaching status once you go through the application process with the IfL. The teaching status of *Associate Teacher Learning and Skills (ATLS)* is for Associate teachers; *Qualified Teacher Learning and Skills (QTLS)* is for Full teachers.

You can register your intent to apply for your teaching status via the IfL website at www.ifl.ac.uk. You will then have a deadline to meet and upload your certificates, complete the online form and obtain your mentor's (or another relevant person's) supporting testimony. Your application will be reviewed and you will be informed if you have been successful. If you have, you will receive an electronic certificate denoting your ATLS or QTLS status. This certificate is your Licence to Practise. However, you must carry out continuing professional development to keep it current, which is evidenced yearly to the IfL via their Reflect website.

Activity

How can you identify what your teaching role will consist of to determine if you will be an Associate or a Full teacher? Have a look at the IfL website www.ifl.ac.uk and familiarise yourself with the ATLS/QTLS application process for your Licence to Practise.

Summary

In this chapter you have learnt about:

- The Institute for Learning

- The minimum core

- Associate and Qualified Teacher status

Theory focus

References and further information

IfL (2008) *Code of Professional Practice*. London: Institute for Learning.

IfL (2009) *Code of Professional Practice: raising concerns about IfL members*. London: Institute for Learning.

LLUK (2006) *New overarching professional standards for teachers, tutors and trainers in the Lifelong Learning Sector*. London: LLUK.

LLUK (2007) *Addressing Literacy, Language, Numeracy and ICT needs in Education and Training: Defining the Minimum Core of Teachers' Knowledge, Understanding and Personal Skills*. London: Lifelong Learning UK.

LLUK (2007) *Inclusive learning approaches for literacy, language, numeracy and ICT: Companion Guide to the Minimum Core*. London: Lifelong Learning UK.

Tummons, J (2010) *Becoming a professional tutor in the Lifelong Learning Sector* (2nd edition). Exeter: Learning Matters.

Websites

Computing free online learning – http://learn.go-on.co.uk/

Further Education Teachers' Qualifications (England) Regulations (2007) – www.legislation.gov.uk/si/si2007/20072264.htm

Further Education Teachers' Qualifications (Wales) – http://tiny.cc/o8who

Institute for Learning – www.ifl.ac.uk

Institute for Learning Code of Professional Practice – www.ifl.ac.uk/membership/professional-standards/code-of-professional-practice

IfL ATLS/QTLS application – www.ifl.ac.uk/cpd/qtls-atls/how-to-apply

IfL Reflect – www.ifl.ac.uk/cpd/reflect

IfL (Summer 2011) *Intuition* – www.ifl.ac.uk/_data/assets/pdffile/0016/25009/IFL-InTuition-Issue-5-Final-Web4.pdf

Learning and Skills Improvement Service – www.lsis.org.uk

Literacy and numeracy free online learning – www.move-on.org.uk

Minimum Core accepted qualifications – http://tinyurl.com/cka789u

Professional Standards for Lecturers in Scotland – http://tiny.cc/3w9jg

Teaching Qualifications for Northern Ireland – http://tiny.cc/2bexb

Introduction

In this chapter you will learn about:
- continuing professional development
- reflection and evaluation
- what next?

Continuing professional development

Continuing professional development (CPD) is all about keeping yourself up to date with changes and developments in your specialist subject area, as well as the theory and practice of teaching. If you are registered with the Institute for Learning (IfL), CPD is a condition in maintaining your Licence to Practise. There are constant changes in education; therefore it is crucial to keep up to date not only for yourself but to benefit your students. Examples include changes to the content of the qualifications you will teach, changes to policies and practices within your organisation and regulatory requirements and government policies. Your organisation may have a strategy for CPD which will prioritise activities they consider are important to improving standards. They might have in-house training events or give you time off to attend external events. CPD can be formal or informal, planned well in advance or be opportunistic, but it should have a real impact upon your teaching role. Ideally, a link should be made through your teaching practice to the ways in which your students have benefited as a result.

If you are working towards Associate or Qualified Teacher status in the Learning and Skills Sector (ATLS/QTLS), you must evidence your CPD annually. This is a requirement of belonging to the Institute for Learning (IfL). The requirement is currently 30 hours a year, or less depending upon how many hours you teach. Once you have achieved your ATLS or QTLS status and have your Licence to Practise, this will be maintained by your taking part in relevant CPD activities. The IfL states that:

> CPD, in relation to a teacher, means continuing professional development, which is any activity undertaken for the purposes of updating knowledge of the subject taught and developing teaching skills.

(IfL, 2007: 2)

Opportunities for professional development include:

- attending events and training programmes
- attending meetings
- e-learning activities
- evaluating feedback from peers and students
- improving own skills such as language, literacy, numeracy and ICT
- membership of professional associations or committees
- observing colleagues
- researching developments or changes to your subject and/or relevant legislation
- secondments
- self-reflection
- shadowing colleagues
- standardisation activities
- studying for relevant qualifications
- subscribing to and reading relevant journals and websites
- visiting other organisations
- voluntary work
- work experience placements
- writing or reviewing books and articles

It's important to maintain records of your CPD, and reflect upon how it has impacted on your teaching role, as the IfL will monitor and sample a selection of their members' CPD records. You can do this via the IfL website, your organisation's systems, or your own manual or electronic records. Maintaining your CPD will ensure that you are not only competent at your job role, but also up to date with the latest developments regarding your specialist subject.

If you are currently teaching, working towards the relevant teaching qualifications will help you contribute towards your CPD, as well as improving your knowledge and skills.

The CPD record you maintain can be a list of what you did and when, and how it has contributed towards your teaching role and specialist subject. You will also need to reflect further regarding the impact each event has had upon your job role. You could use a record like the one in the example overleaf, and then keep separate records of your reflections along with your notes, minutes of meetings and records of attendance. These could be given a reference number and filed for future access or for IfL sampling. Alternatively, you can use the IfL's online recording system called *Reflect* to maintain your record as well as your reflections. Always keep a copy of any documentation relating to your training and CPD, as you may need to provide this to funding, awarding organisation or regulatory bodies if requested.

Example of a CPD record

Continuing professional development record					
Name: Marie Brown		Organisation: Excellence Training College		IfL number: AAOOII22	
Date	Activity and venue	Duration	Justification towards teaching role and subject specialism	Further training needs	Ref no
II May 2012	Attendance at college standardisation event. We discussed how we interpreted the requirements of unit 301, how we each taught and assessed it and then we reassessed each other's decisions.	3 hrs	Standardised teaching and assessment practice to ensure I am assessing unit 301 in the same way as the other assessors.	Unit 302 to be reviewed at the next meeting	I
23 June 2012	Attendance at a First Aid training day at the local community hall.	6 hrs	To ensure I am current with First Aid in case someone has an accident.	–	2
20 July 2012	Attendance at staff training event for all assessors at college. We were able to get together and discuss the documents and records we use as these have recently been updated. We were also given updates regarding the college's policies and procedures.	3 hrs	This ensured I am up to date with college documents and procedures regarding assessment practice.	–	3

You can update your CPD record at any time. However, if you are registered with the IfL, you will need to declare your CPD annually and they will e-mail you a reminder beforehand.

You will probably participate in an appraisal or performance review system at your organisation. This is a valuable opportunity to discuss your learning, development and any training or support you may need in the future. It is also a chance to reflect upon your achievements and successes. Having the support of your organisation will help you decide what is relevant to your development as a teacher, your job role and your specialist subject. You could share your ideas with colleagues if it's something everyone could benefit from.

Keeping up to date

Once you have your Licence to Practise, you are classed as a *dual professional*. This means you are a professional teacher, as well as a professional in your specialist subject area.

The following websites are useful to help you keep up to date with information regarding developments in the Lifelong Learning Sector. Most of them will allow you to register for regular electronic updates. You could also join professional networks where you will find groups you can join specifically aimed at your specialist subject or the qualification you will teach.

Department for Business, Innovation and Skills – www.bis.gov.uk
Department for Education – www.education.gov.uk
Equality and Diversity Forum – www.edf.org.uk
Government updates: Education and Learning – www.direct.gov.uk/en/
    EducationAndLearning/index.htm
Institute for Learning – www.ifl.ac.uk
Learning and Skills Improvement Service – www.lsis.org.uk
National Institute of Adult Continuing Education – www.niace.org.uk
Ofqual – www.ofqual.gov.uk/
Ofsted – www.ofsted.gov.uk
PCET– www.pcet.net
Times Educational Supplement Online - www.tes.co.uk

Legislation and codes of practice

It is important for you to keep up to date with all relevant legislation and codes of practice to ensure you are remaining current with your knowledge and practice, and any changes or updates that have taken place. These can be grouped into *generic* i.e. relating to your role as a teacher, and *specific*, i.e. relating to the specialist subject you will teach.

Generic

Your own organisation will have relevant codes of practice such as disciplinary, conduct, dress, timekeeping and sustainability. There will also be policies and procedures to follow such as appeals, complaints, and risk assessments, etc. If you are employed, you will have received a contract of employment and perhaps an employee handbook which should state your organisation's rules and procedures. These will differ depending upon the context and environment within which you will teach. You also need to be aware of the requirements of external bodies and regulators such as Ofsted (in England), who inspect provision, along with awarding organisations, who will quality assure their qualifications, and funding agencies, who will need data and statistics.

The following information was current at the time of writing. However, you are advised to check for any changes or updates, and whether they are applicable outside England.

The following are examples of generic legislation and codes of practice.

- Code of Professional Practice (2008) introduced by the Institute for Learning (IfL) to cover the activities of teachers in the Lifelong Learning Sector. The Code is based on seven behaviours:
  - Professional integrity
  - Respect
  - Reasonable care
  - Professional practice
  - Criminal offence disclosure
  - Responsibility during Institute investigations
  - Responsibility to the Institute

- Copyright, Designs and Patents Act (1988) relates to the copying, adapting and distributing of materials, which includes computer programs and materials obtained via the internet. Your organisation may have a licence to enable you to photocopy small amounts from books or journals. Anything you do copy should be acknowledged, i.e. by giving the details of the original author and text.

- Data Protection Act (2003) made provision for the regulation of the processing of information relating to individuals, including the obtaining, holding, use or disclosure of such information. The records you have regarding your students will be covered by this Act.

- Equality Act (2010) replaced all previous anti-discrimination legislation and consolidated it into one act (England, Scotland and Wales). It provides rights for people not to be directly discriminated against or harassed because they have an *association* with a disabled person, nor must people be directly discriminated against or harassed because they are wrongly *perceived* as disabled. Reasonable adjustments must take place during teaching and learning activities to lessen or remove the effects of a disadvantage to a student with a disability. The Act identifies nine *protected characteristics* which refers to aspects of a person's identity which are protected from discrimination. They are:
  - age
  - disability
  - gender
  - gender identity
  - marriage and civil partnership
  - maternity and pregnancy
  - race

– religion and belief

– sexual orientation

- Freedom of Information Act (2000) gives people the opportunity to request to see the information public authorities hold about them.

- Health and Safety at Work etc. Act (1974) imposes obligations on all staff within an organisation commensurate with their role and responsibility. Risk assessments should be carried out where necessary. In the event of an accident, particularly one resulting in death or serious injury, an investigation by the Health and Safety Executive may result in the prosecution of individuals found to be negligent as well as the organisation.

- Protection of Children Act (POCA) (1999) was designed to protect children. It gives responsibility to local authorities to make enquiries when anyone contacts them with concerns about child abuse. You will need to be checked by the Criminal Records Bureau (CRB) before you can teach children or vulnerable adults.

- Safeguarding Vulnerable Groups Act (2006) introduced a vetting and barring scheme to make decisions about who should be barred from working with children and vulnerable adults. You may need to have a CRB check before you can teach.

- The Further Education Teachers' Qualifications (England) Regulations (2007) brought in revised teaching qualifications for new teachers and a professional status for all teachers in the Further Education Sector in England. Teachers must register with the Institute for Learning (IfL) and partake in continuing professional development (CPD). Teachers should be qualified and hold ATLS or QTLS status within five years of starting a teaching position.

Specific

These will differ depending upon the subject and environment within which you teach.

The following are examples of specific legislation and codes of practice.

- Control of Substances Hazardous to Health (COSHH) Regulations (2002) apply to working with hazardous materials.

- Food Hygiene Regulations (2006) apply to aspects of farming, manufacturing, distributing and retailing food.

- Information Technology Codes of Practice relate to the use of computers in your particular organisation, for example, internet access and e-mail protocol.

- Management of Health and Safety at Work Regulations (1999) aim to prevent unsafe practices and minimise risks, for example, the use of visual displays.

- Manual Handling Operation Regulations (1992) relate to hazards of manual handling and risks of injury.

- Reporting of Injuries, Diseases and Dangerous Occurrences (RIDDOR) Regulations (1995) ensure specified workplace incidents are reported.

Following the required legislation and codes of practice and carrying out your roles and responsibilities to the best of your ability will help ensure you become an effective and professional teacher.

Activity

Decide on a method for documenting your CPD. You could use a form like the example in this chapter, or you could design your own. Consider what activities would be relevant to your specialist subject or teaching in general. If you have carried out some CPD, reflect upon each activity by considering how it will impact upon your teaching role. A useful CPD activity could be to research the legislation and codes of practice relevant to the specialist subject you will be teaching.

Reflection and evaluation

Self-reflection is a good way of continually evaluating your own practice to ensure you are carrying out your role effectively. When doing this, you need to consider how your own attitude and behaviour have impacted upon others, particularly your students, and what you could do to improve yourself.

Reflection is often just your thoughts, which can be positive or negative but can take into account any feedback you have received. It is useful to keep a learning journal to note anything important; you can then refer to this when planning your future development or preparing your teaching sessions. Reflection is about becoming more self-aware, which should give you increased confidence and improve the links between the theory and practice of teaching. It's useful to complete a journal after each session you teach to help you focus on what went well and what you could improve upon. An example of a learning journal is given on page 83.

A straightforward method of reflection is to have an **e**xperience, then **d**escribe it, **a**nalyse it and **r**evise it (EDAR). This method incorporates the who, what, when, where, why and how approach (WWWWWH) and should help you consider ways of changing and/or improving.

Experience → Describe → Analyse → Revise (EDAR)

(Gravells and Simpson, 2008: 90)

Example

Learning Journal	
Name: *Devra Cohen*	**Date:** *20 April 2012*

Experience *significant event or incident*	*Yesterday was the first session with a new group and I felt it didn't go according to plan. I focused too much on what I wanted to teach and too little on how and what the group wanted to learn.* *Some of the students interrupted me to ask questions, which reduced the amount of time I had to get through everything.*
Describe *who, what, when, where*	*There were 12 students aged 17 to 60 attending a six-week daytime programme on flower arranging from 2–5 p.m. The session took place in a workshop with windows that wouldn't open and not enough chairs. The water supply to the sink had been switched off therefore I couldn't clean up properly at the end. Some students arrived and asked questions while I was setting up the room, which delayed me.*
Analyse *why, how (impact on teaching and learning)*	*I should have arrived earlier to check that the water was switched on, and to obtain extra chairs. My students got rather warm during the session as there was no fresh air. Had I sorted this prior to the students arriving they would not have known of the problems. The class would then have started promptly and I would not have felt flustered.* *I had too much paperwork to get through. The students had to fill in an enrolment form, I needed to carry out an initial assessment of their prior learning and ascertain if anyone had any particular needs. I also wanted them to take a learning styles test but there wasn't enough time. I had a list of things I wanted to get through, including an icebreaker and agreeing the ground rules, but I forgot to agree the ground rules as I was rushing things. As a result I feel I looked unprofessional.* *The icebreaker went well but was a bit hurried due to the late start. I had an induction checklist which kept me focused, but it was 3.45 p.m. before I realised the students needed a break. By this time, some of them were not paying attention to me but talking to others.* *I feel not much learning took place as I was focusing too much on the paperwork and programme requirements. I had three flower arrangements I wanted to show them how to create but we only had time for one.*
Revise *changes and/or improvements required*	*I will arrive earlier to ensure the room is ready and allow more time for questions when preparing my session plan. I will ask what the students' expectations are and explain how I can meet them. We will set the ground rules next week.* *In future, I will interview all students in advance and ask them to complete the enrolment form, learning styles test and an initial assessment prior to their commencing. This will help me ascertain all the information I need to help plan my first session, and make it go more smoothly. I have reported the windows to the caretaker.* *I have realised the first session is not about me and the paperwork I need to complete, but about what the students want to know and learn about the subject.*

- Experience – a significant event or incident you would like to change or improve.

- Describe – aspects such as who was involved, what happened, when it happened and where it happened.

- Analyse – consider the experience more deeply and ask yourself how it happened and why it happened.

- Revise – think about how you would handle it differently if it happened again and then try this out if you have the opportunity.

As a result, you might find you improve your own skills by, for example, giving more effective, constructive and developmental feedback to your students.

Reflection should become a habit; for example, mentally running through the EDAR points after a significant event, or completing a journal. As you become more experienced and analytical with reflective practice, you will progress from thoughts of *I didn't do that very well,* to aspects of more significance such as *why* you didn't do it very well and *how* you could change something as a result. You may realise you need further training or support in some areas, therefore partaking in relevant CPD should help.

Part of reflection is about knowing what you need to change and why. If you are not aware of some aspect that needs changing, you will continue as you are until something more serious occurs.

The IfL states:

> *The activities you choose as relevant to you and your practice will only count as CPD if:*
>
> - *you can critically reflect on what you have learned;*
> - *you can evidence how you have applied this to your practice;*
> - *you can evidence how this has impacted on your learners' experience and success.*

(IfL, 2007: 9)

Maintaining your CPD, keeping up to date with developments in your subject area and changes in legislation and qualification standards will assist your knowledge and practice. Whatever you do should have a real, positive impact upon your students and their learning.

Evaluation

Whichever type of programme you teach, short- or long-term, it is important to evaluate the teaching and learning process. This should be an ongoing procedure throughout all aspects of the teaching and learning cycle. It will help you realise how effective you were and what you could change or improve, for example, using different types of resources. It will also help you identify any problem areas, enabling you to do things differently next time. Using feedback from others, information and data is the best way to evaluate the programme you have taught. Never assume everything is going well just because you think it is.

Obtaining feedback

Feedback can come from surveys and questionnaires, reviews, appraisals and informal and formal discussions and meetings. Other information to help you evaluate your programme includes statistics such as achievement and destinations, which can affect the amount of funding received by your organisation. All feedback should help evaluate whether teaching and learning have been successful (or not) as well as help you to improve your own practice and inform future planning.

If you have taught a one-day or short programme, you might give your students a questionnaire at the end. Always build in time into your session for this to take place, otherwise your students may take away the questionnaire and forget to return it. It could contain closed questions such as: *Were the teaching and learning approaches suitable? Yes/No,* or open questions such as: *How did you find the teaching and learning approaches?* The latter is best as you should gain more information. When issuing questionnaires, decide whether or not you want the responses to be anonymous as you might gain more feedback if students know they cannot be identified.

You might decide to use a mixture of open and closed questions. Open questions always require a full response and give you *qualitative data* to work with; closed questions only elicit a *yes* or *no* answer and give you *quantitative data*. If you use a closed question, follow this up with an open question to enable you to obtain further information.

Example

1   *Did the programme fulfil your expectations? Yes/No*
    How or why was this?
2   *Were the teaching methods and resources appropriate? Yes/No*
    Why was this?
3   *Was the venue suitable? Yes/No*
    What did/didn't you like about it?
4   *Did you enjoy your learning experience? Yes/No*
    What did/didn't you like?
5   *Have you gained the skills and knowledge you expected to? Yes/No*
    What improvements would you recommend for the future?

There are many ways of writing questions to gain different types of responses. A closed question could be followed by a response scale of 1–5 for students to circle (one being *no* or *low*, five being *yes* or *high*), for example:

Did the programme fulfil your expectations? 1 2 3 4 5

The tendency might be to choose number 3 as it is in the middle. Removing a number makes the response more definitive one way or the other, for example:

Did the programme fulfil your expectations? 1 2 3 4

Instead of numbers, you could use smiley faces for students to circle, for example:

Did the programme fulfil your expectations? ☹ ☺ ☺

Whatever you decide to ask, make sure you keep your questions simple, for instance, don't ask two questions in one sentence or use complicated jargon. Always allow space for written responses and thank your students for their contributions. Ensure you analyse the responses and inform your students of how their contributions have led to changes and improvements.

Talking to your students informally will help you realise how successful your teaching has been. This can be done during reviews, at break times or before or after your sessions. Your students are the best judges of whether they are getting what they feel they need. If given the opportunity, they may give you more feedback in an informal situation.

If you are teaching a longer programme, it is useful to obtain feedback partway through, as well as at the end. This will enable you to make any necessary changes. Evaluation and feedback can contribute to your organisation's quality assurance by helping improve the service given to students.

Activity

Design a short questionnaire that you could use with your own students in the future. Consider what information you would like to know and why, and then write your questions carefully. If you are already teaching and have the opportunity, use it with your students, analyse the results and decide on an action plan for improvements. Don't forget to inform your students of any changes as a result.

What next?

Hopefully, you have now decided to become a teacher in the Lifelong Learning Sector (LLS) and would like to work towards a teaching qualification or gain some teaching practice. To become a qualified teacher in the LLS you need to begin by achieving the Award in Preparing to Teach in the Lifelong Learning Sector (PTLLS) at level 3 or 4. This is mandatory if you will be teaching in Further Education or teaching on government-funded programmes in England. You can then progress towards a relevant teaching qualification, which will depend upon your job role as either an *Associate* or *Full* teacher (see Chapter 4 for details). An Associate teacher does not carry out or have the responsibilities that a Full teacher would, i.e. they might teach programmes where someone else has designed the scheme of work, session plans and resources. Associate teachers must take the Certificate in Teaching in the Lifelong Learning Sector (CTLLS) at level 3 or 4. Full teachers must take the Diploma in Teaching in the Lifelong Learning Sector (DTTLS), also known as the Certificate in Education or Post/Professional Graduate Certificate in Education (PGCE) at level 5 or above.

Both CTLLS and DTLLS contain units which can be taken over a period of time. It might take up to one year to achieve CTLLS and up to two years to achieve DTLLS. The units you will have achieved from the PTLLS Award will be counted towards both CTLLS and DTLLS. For both qualifications, you need to be in a teaching role and evidence a certain number of teaching practice hours, for example, 30 for CTLLS and 100 for DTLLS. If you move to a different area of the country while working towards your qualifications, the units you have already achieved should be saved on your QCF record, therefore you don't have to start the teaching qualification again, you can just pick up where you left off. This is providing the units have successfully been claimed by the organisation you were attending. You will receive a unit certificate which must be produced as evidence.

To become fully qualified and licensed to teach in the Lifelong Learning Sector, you will need to:

- register with the Institute for Learning (IfL) within six months of starting your teaching role
- complete the PTLLS Award within one year
- complete CTLLS *or* DTLLS/Cert Ed/PGCE within five years (which includes the PTLLS Award time)
- achieve or evidence the Minimum Core (to at least Level 2)
- carry out a period of professional formation in a teaching role
- demonstrate an ongoing commitment to continuing professional development (CPD)
- apply to the IfL for ATLS or QTLS status depending upon your job role

Other appropriate qualifications

There are many organisations which offer short *Train the Trainer* programmes. These might last one or two days, or a few days or a week, and are designed to give you an introduction to training, usually in the workplace. They are not accepted as being equivalent to the PTLLS Award but they will give you a good grounding in the basics of how to teach and train others.

If you are training in organisations or in the workplace it may be appropriate for you to work towards a Learning and Development qualification as opposed to a teaching qualification. However, you will need to check what the requirements are for your subject and organisation. The Learning and Development qualifications are made up of units just like the teaching qualifications, and some units are interchangeable between them. These qualifications are achieved by demonstrating your competence in your training role at work.

If you will be assessing your students, you might need to gain an Assessor Award. If you are quality assuring the practice of other assessors, you might need to gain a Quality Assurer Award. Please see Chapter 2 for further details of both. Some qualifications require their assessors and quality assurers to hold specific qualifications whereas others just expect the staff to have knowledge and experience. To find out if you need to be qualified, you could obtain a syllabus for the particular qualification you will assess or quality assure and check the staffing requirements. These are usually available from awarding organisations' websites.

Voluntary work

If you don't have a teaching position at present, a good way of finding out if you do want to teach is to carry out some voluntary work. You could contact your local college or training organisation and ask if you could volunteer to work alongside an existing teacher. This would help you see how classes are structured and taught in your specialist subject area. You could also ask if you could observe teachers in different subjects from your own. This would give you ideas for different teaching and learning activities you might like to use in the future. However, some organisations might not be able to take volunteers due to health and safety or security reasons. If you are currently teaching (paid or voluntary), you should have a mentor whom you would be able to observe. Equally, they could observe you and give you feedback to help your development.

Teaching in schools

At some point, you may decide to move out of the Lifelong Learning Sector and into a different area such as teaching in a school or academy. Currently, in

England and Wales teachers in schools maintained by local authorities should have Qualified Teacher Status (QTS) by achieving a degree in their specialist subject and a Postgraduate Certificate in Education (PGCE). Teachers in independent schools are not required to hold QTS, although most do prefer teachers to hold this status unless they have significant teaching experience. Some teacher training schemes allow graduates to teach in schools without a PGCE after an intense period of training. At the time of publication, the IfL were looking into progression opportunities for Qualified Teacher Learning and Skills (QTLS) teachers to be able to teach in a school without holding QTS status. However, a school is a different environment and different skills are required to teach younger age ranges. You might therefore like to attend further training or take units of a relevant teaching qualification to help you.

The Wolf Report (2011) put forward proposals to recognise QTLS status within schools. Toni Fazaeli, IfL's Chief Executive, said:

> The government's confirmation that it will legislate for holders of QTLS to teach in schools is a major victory for further education teachers, who have long sought parity with their school sector colleagues, and will improve the career opportunities for those with QTLS status.
>
> (IfL press release, 13 May 2011)
>
> www.ifl.ac.uk/newsandevents/press-releases/ifl-welcomes-commitment-to-strengthening-vocational-education (accessed 8 June 2011)

Hopefully, you will now pursue a career in teaching in the Lifelong Learning Sector, whether full-time or part-time. This will enable you to make a difference to many people's lives, offering you an extremely rewarding career.

Activity

Create an action plan for yourself with the following headings: aims, action required and target date. List all your aims which relate to obtaining a teaching position, for example, achieving the PTLLS Award. Research how you can achieve your aims and set yourself target dates for each.

Summary

In this chapter you have learnt about:

- continuing professional development
- reflection and evaluation
- what next?

Theory focus

References and further information

DfE (2011) *Review of Vocational Education – The Wolf Report*. DFE-00031-2011.

Gravells, A (2012) *Preparing to Teach in the Lifelong Learning Sector* (5th edition). London: Learning Matters.

Gravells, A and Simpson, S (2008) *Planning and Enabling Learning in the Lifelong Learning Sector* (1st edition). Exeter: Learning Matters.

Institute for Learning (2007) *Guidelines for your continuing professional development (CPD)*. London: IfL.

Institute for Learning (2010) *Brilliant teaching and training in FE and skills: A guide to effective CPD for teachers, trainers and leaders*. London: Learning and Skills Improvement Service.

Roffey-Barenstsen, J and Malthouse, R (2009) *Reflective Practice in the Lifelong Learning Sector*. Exeter: Learning Matters.

Websites

Ann Gravells (information regarding teaching) – www.anngravells.co.uk

Institute for Learning: gaining ATLS/QTLS – www.ifl.ac.uk/cpd/qtls-atls

Institute for Learning: CPD – www.ifl.ac.uk/cpd

Institute for Learning: Reflect – www.ifl.ac.uk/cpd/reflect

Government legislation – www.legislation.gov.uk

Qualifications and Credit Framework shortcut – http://tinyurl.com/447bgy2

Training and Development Agency for Schools (TDA) – www.tda.gov.uk

APPENDIX I
LIFELONG LEARNING SECTOR ABBREVIATIONS AND ACRONYMS

AB	Awarding Body
ACE	Adult and Continuing Education
ACL	Adult and Community Learning
AO	Awarding Organisation
AoC	Association of Colleges
ATLS	Associate Teacher Learning and Skills
BIS	Department for Business, Innovation and Skills
CCEA	Council for the Curriculum, Examinations and Assessment (Northern Ireland)
CIEA	Chartered Institute of Educational Assessors
COSHH	Control of Substances Hazardous to Health
CPD	Continuing Professional Development
CTLLS	Certificate in Teaching in the Lifelong Learning Sector
DCELLS	Department for Children, Education, Lifelong Learning and Skills (Wales)
DfE	Department for Education
DTLLS	Diploma in Teaching in the Lifelong Learning Sector
EDAR	Experience, describe, analyse and revise
EQA	External Quality Assurer
FE	Further Education
FENTO	Further Education National Training Organisation
FETC	Further Education Teachers' Certificate
FEU	Further Education Unit
GLH	Guided learning hours
GCSE	General Certificate of Secondary Education
GTC	General Teaching Council
HE	Higher Education
ICT	Information Communication Technology
IfL	Institute for Learning
ILP	Individual learning plan
ITT/ITE	Initial teacher training/initial teacher education
IQA	Internal Quality Assurer/Assurance
LLS	Lifelong Learning Sector
LLUK	Lifelong Learning UK
LSIS	Learning and Skills Improvement Service

NAS	National Apprenticeship Service
NEET	Not in employment, education or training
NIACE	National Institute of Adult Continuing Education
NOS	National Occupational Standards
NCVQ	National Council for Vocational Qualifications
NVQ	National Vocational Qualification
Ofqual	Office of Qualifications and Examinations Regulation
Ofsted	Office for Standards in Education, Children's Services and Skills
PCET	Post Compulsory Education and Training
PGCE	Postgraduate Certificate in Education
PTLLS	Preparing to Teach in the Lifelong Learning Sector
QCA	Qualifications and Curriculum Authority
QCDA	Qualifications and Curriculum Development Agency
QCF	Qualifications and Credit Framework
QTS	Qualified Teacher Status (schools)
QTLS	Qualified Teacher Learning and Skills
RARPA	Recognising and recording progress and achievement
RoC	Rules of combination
RPL	Recognition of prior learning
RWE	Realistic working environment
SCN	Scottish Candidate Number
SCQF	Scottish Credit and Qualifications Framework
SfA	Skills Funding Agency
SMART	Specific, measurable, achievable, realistic and time bound
SQA	Scottish Qualifications Authority
SSB	Standard Setting Body
SSC	Sector Skills Council
SVUK	Standards Verification UK
SWOT	Strengths, weaknesses, opportunities and threats
TAQA	Training, assessment and quality assurance
TDLB	Training and Development Lead Body
UCET	Universities Council for the Education of Teachers
UKCES	UK Commission for Employment and Skills
ULN	Unique learner number
VACSR	Valid, authentic, current, sufficient, reliable
VARK	Visual, aural, read/write, kinaesthetic
VET	Vocational education and training
VLE	Virtual learning environment
VQ	Vocational Qualification
WEA	Workers' Educational Association
WBL	Work-based learning
WWWWWH	Who, what, when, where, why and how
YPLA	Young People's Learning Agency

1. What is the Lifelong Learning Sector?

It is the term used for the educational provision for those aged 14 and above taking a purposeful learning activity with the aim of improving or furthering their skills and knowledge.

2. Do I need to be a qualified teacher before I can apply for a teaching position?

In most instances, you do not need to be a qualified teacher when you apply for a teaching position. You can take an introduction to teaching programme before you commence a teaching role, just to find out if you are suited to it and whether it's what you would like to do. This is known as the Award in Preparing to Teach in the Lifelong Learning Sector (PTLLS). You can also work towards a relevant teaching qualification when you first start teaching.

3. How will I know if teaching is for me, I don't feel very confident yet?

You can take a short *Train the Trainer* programme. This is usually one or two days and will give you an insight into what it's like to teach and train others. The PTLLS Award is the first part of the recognised teacher training qualifications and introduces you to all aspects of teaching and assessing. Attendance is often flexible and the programme is offered nationally. You will be required to deliver a session to your peer group, which might seem a bit daunting but it will help build your confidence and give you an idea if teaching is for you.

You do not need to be in a teaching role to take the Train the Trainer programme or PTLLS Award. However, it's useful if you have a subject in mind that you would like to teach.

You could also ask at local training centres and colleges if they offer the programmes. Additonally you could ask if you could observe a few teaching sessions in your subject area to see what it's like.

4. What qualifications do I need to take?

You can start with the PTLLS Award, then progress to the Certificate in Teaching in the Lifelong Learning Sector (CTLLS). This qualification is for *associate teachers*, i.e. those teaching mainly from materials prepared by others. If you are classed as a *full teacher*, i.e. teaching using materials you have prepared yourself, you will progress to the Diploma in Teaching in the Lifelong Learning Sector (DTLLS) after taking PTLLS.

DTLLS is also known as the Certificate in Education. If you have a degree, you can take the Postgraduate Certificate in Education/Professional Graduate Certificate in Education which are at a higher level.

You must be aged 19 or over to take any of these qualifications.

5. Do I need to be qualified in the subject I want to teach?

It will depend upon what your subject is and whether your students will be taking a qualification or just learning for pleasure. Some subjects do require you to be qualified whereas others require you to be knowledgeable and/or experienced. The organisation you apply to teach for will be able to tell you.

6. Who pays for my teaching qualification?

If you have already started teaching, your employer might fund it for you. If not, you will need to pay for it yourself. However, there might be a grant or a loan that you could apply for. There might even be a bursary available from a university or government department if there is a shortage of teachers in your subject area. See www.ifl.ac.uk/membership/initial-teacher-training-itt for details.

7. How long will it take to get qualified?

The PTLLS Award, which everyone must start with in England, can take from a few days to a few months depending upon where you enrol. CTLLS can take from a few months up to a year and DTLLS from one year to two years. You will need to find out which organisations are offering the qualifications in your area and ask them how long they last. Even though the content is the same wherever you take the qualification, the time frames can differ, i.e. if some are intensive programmes or combine online learning with attendance.

Once you have your qualification you will undertake a probation period known as professional formation. You can then apply for Associate or Qualified Teacher Learning and Skills (ATLS/QTLS) status through the Institute for Learning (IfL). This must be within five years of starting as a teacher. You will need to achieve or evidence your literacy and numeracy skills to at least Level 2. Details can be found at www.ifl.ac.uk/cpd/qtls-atls

8. What will I have to do to pass the qualifications?

You will need to evidence all the assessment criteria contained in the various units of the qualifications you are taking. This is usually by a combination of assignments, essays, teaching practice and written statements. You will need at least 30 teaching practice hours for CTLLS and 100 for DTLLS. You will need to be supported by a mentor, another teacher in your subject area. You will be observed teaching some of your sessions to your students.

9. How much reading and research will I have to do?

This will depend upon whether you aim to achieve CTLLS or DTLLS. Each unit in the qualification has a number of hours allocated for contact with a teacher and for self-study. For example, the PTLLS unit, *Roles, Responsibilities and Relationships in Lifelong Learning* is a total of 30 hours, on average 12 with a teacher and 18 for self-study. This is just an average and you might not need the full amount. You will need to do some reading; however, you might not need to read all the chapters of all the textbooks on the reading list. Your teacher will advise you which books are the best to refer to. You can then look up relevant aspects in the index to locate the information you need at that point in time. The internet is also a valuable research tool; however, you should not rely totally on it.

10. I haven't taken an academic qualification before, how difficult will it be?

Once you enrol for your programme, you should be given support regarding what is required and how to approach the different assessment activities. There are lots of textbooks regarding how to study and write in an academic way. If you find something difficult, just talk to your teacher, they are there to help you.

11. What skills do I need as a teacher?

Besides having the skills and knowledge regarding the subject you will teach, you need to be passionate about your subject and be able to communicate this to others. This will help towards your enthusiasm to teach and your students' motivation to learn. You also need to have patience, organisational and time management skills. If you don't already have numeracy and literacy to Level 2, you will need to take these before applying for your teaching status. Computing skills are also required as so much technology is used today, not only for teaching, but for administrative purposes.

12. I've taught in a school, can I now teach in a college?

If you have Qualified Teacher Status (QTS) you should be able to teach in a college without retaking any teaching qualifications. You would need to undertake a probation period known as *professional formation* and then apply for Qualified Teacher Learning and Skills (QTLS) status through the Institute for Learning (IfL) within two years of starting teaching.

13. If I qualify to teach in the Lifelong Learning Sector and gain my QTLS status, can I then change my mind and teach in a school or an academy?

Yes, this may be possible. At the time of writing, new guidelines were being produced as a result of the recommendations in the Wolf Report (2011).

14. How secure are teaching jobs in the LLS?

Unfortunately, it is very rare that a teaching job can be guaranteed as secure. You could be employed on a permanent or temporary contract basis as a part-time or full-time teacher. Alternatively, you might just be paid by the sessions you teach, or you might be training an employee on the job, which is part of your job description anyway. All teaching contracts differ, therefore you will need to find out the terms and conditions when you apply for a teaching position.

15. What will I get paid?

Pay in the Lifelong Learning Sector varies widely. It will differ depending upon how you are employed, i.e. temporary, permanent, full-time, part-time, sessional, etc. Full-time teachers in colleges are paid on average £15,000–£36,000 per annum. Hourly-paid teachers and assessors can expect to be paid between £10 and £25 per hour. This all depends upon the subject to be taught, where it is taught and the qualifications held.

16. How can I make my sessions interesting?

Try and use different activities which suit your students, i.e. a mixture of input from yourself, talking, group work, presentations, paired work, discussions, practical tasks, etc. Once you get to know your students you will know what works and what doesn't and it will also depend upon what resources are available to you. Don't be afraid to try something different (as long as it's safe) and check that learning is taking place by regularly asking questions, using quizzes, practical tasks and observing what is happening.

17. How can I stop my students getting bored?

Often, students are bored because they switch off for some reason. This could be that they are not challenged enough, or because they feel they are getting left behind. If you have a student who is doing well, set them some harder tasks, if you have a student who is falling behind, set them an easier task which you know they can achieve. You can then set them a slightly harder task until they build up their confidence. You may have students of different levels within the same group, therefore you need to differentiate the learning process. Students also get bored if they are asked to do something which they feel is not relevant. Try and use anecdotes and stories to bring your subject to life.

18. How can I control behaviour and disruption?

You will experience lots of different situations throughout your teaching career. For example, a student interrupts you to ask a pertinent question, or other students talk among themselves while you are talking. You will need to remain calm, but be assertive in your response. For example, if students are talking over you, stop talking and wait. Look at them until they stop and then, using eye contact, say 'Thank you' in an assertive but not sarcastic tone. It's really only with experience that you will find what works and what doesn't. However, there are lots of good textbooks on behaviour which you could refer to.

Reading lists in picture format for PTLLS, CTLLS and DTLLS can be found at www.anngravells.co.uk